Celebration

Celebration:
Resources for all-age Eucharists

Margaret Withers and Tony Pinchin

Gracewing.

First published in 1996

Gracewing
Fowler Wright Books
2 Southern Ave, Leominster
Herefordshire HR6 0QF

ISBN 0 85244 348 X

Typesetting by Action Typesetting Ltd,
Gloucester, GL1 1SP

Printed by Cromwell Press
Broughton Gifford, Wiltshire, SN12 8PH

Contents

Introduction: Mr and Mrs Miller and family

Stephen and Jane Miller and their children approach the church with some trepidation. They have come at the invitation of their neighbour who has been gently prodding them to do something about the promises they made five years ago at the baptism of their youngest son, Simon. They have heard from another family down the road that the first Sunday of the month at St Mary's can be quite fun.

On entering the church the Millers are immediately set at their ease by a friendly but not over-pushy greeting in the church porch. Simon gasps with delight as he sees an elephant's trunk poking around a pillar. There is an immediate sense of intrigue as the family spots a giraffe, a bear and a zebra.

Soon someone comes to the microphone and says a word of welcome before beginning to rehearse a repetitive but rather beautiful chant. The Millers have never heard anything like it before, but they soon feel at home singing it. They notice how, when the practice is over, an expectant hush descends on the Brownies and Cubs sitting at the front. Their own children, Simon, James and Rebecca, are sitting still too, which causes them even more surprise. It was the last thing they had expected.

Then the first hymn begins, a well-known one they have heard on *Songs of Praise*, and a procession of various people all dressed up comes in and goes to the front of the church. The priest seems friendly and yet respectful in the way he starts the service. After some singing, which the congregation seems to know, everyone sits down. A reader speaks briefly about the first reading. The animals are to help people imagine they are in Noah's Ark looking out! Simon keeps looking at them and finds there is plenty to watch besides. During the reading about God giving a rainbow as the sign of his love after the flood-waters subsided, a huge coloured rainbow comes up from behind the altar and hangs in mid-air. Everyone is asked to stand and look at the

1

font while water is poured into it and the reader speaks about baptism reminding us of Noah being kept safe during the flood. Then lines of Brownies and Guides appear on the step at the front of the church and the priest explains that they are going to turn around – which is what Jesus says he wants us all to do in the Gospel – something about 'repenting'.

By now the Miller family feel well and truly at home with the people around them. They feel something special about the atmosphere when everyone kneels quietly as the organ plays mysteriously while the priest stands at the altar and sings words about Jesus taking bread and saying, 'This is my body'. Everyone is looking at what is happening and, somehow, they all seem to be involved. Rebecca remembers her teacher at school describing something like this. James recalls being at a similar service one day when he went to church during a Cub camp at the seaside and senses a slight tingle in his spine.

When the Lord's Prayer begins, Jane feels a lump come into her throat as she sees the Junior Church children lift their hands up and sing at the tops of their voices, while Stephen remembers singing it in church as a boy. They are suddenly aware that their children have not fidgeted or whispered to one another at all. When people start going up for Holy Communion a woman gently invites the Millers to go too and they feel that, although they are not receiving the bread and wine, the blessing the priest gives them makes them both involved and welcome.

Soon the last hymn comes, all about learning to pray and serve God better. The Millers, each in their own way, feel somehow different.

Chapter One

Principles

A eucharistic landscape

This book attempts to show how people of all ages and at all stages of spiritual growth can meet and be touched by God, can learn and grow, through the form of worship left to the Church by the Lord Jesus Christ himself – the Eucharist, also known as the Mass or Holy Communion.

Over the past generation there has been a significant change in the pattern of Sunday worship in many churches. In the Roman Catholic Church, the Mass, always the central act of worship, has become more accessible following the liturgical reforms of Vatican II. In the Church of England, the Eucharist has gradually become established in the majority of parishes as the main Sunday service, while in the Free Churches services, including Holy Communion, have become more frequent and children are sometimes welcome at them.

Eucharistic worship with people of all ages present is nothing new in the Church of England. Many parishes have been celebrating such Eucharists for generations with special music, simplified or abbreviated texts and considerable active participation. There are still many churches, however, where a 'not in front of the children' approach has prevailed and where the celebration of Holy Communion is thought to be appropriate for committed Christian adults only. In some Anglican parishes, a non-eucharistic Family Service replaces the usual Parish Eucharist three or four times a year or even monthly.

In other Anglican and most Free churches, the central service is usually a non-eucharistic one. Holy Communion is celebrated once a month after the main service or only on special occasions. Some of these churches have highly creative forms of worship because they have worked hard at introducing congregational participation, drama and visual symbolism out of their concern to present biblical material in an

3

exciting and relevant way. Some of these churches are now keen to develop all-age eucharistic worship, perhaps once or twice a month as their main Sunday service.

In addition to this, there are many people of all ages on the fringe of church life whose experience of churchgoing has never included eucharistic worship. The service left by the Lord, 'Do this in remembrance of me', does not form part of their relationship with him.

The pilgrim people of God

The idea that all ages can worship together has been encouraged by the rediscovery of a model of the Christian community that sees its members as sharing a journey of faith. In the Church of England the General Synod report, *Children in the Way*[1] marked a watershed in thought with its promotion of the model of a Pilgrim Church in which people of different ages and stages of faith development meet and work together. All-age learning and worship is increasingly popular though some individuals and, indeed, whole church communities find that it takes a long time to change the underlying attitude that children and adults should spend most of their church life separated from each other.

Alongside the development of all-age worship there is a growing consensus that it is not only possible but also right for the children of a congregation to be fully included within its eucharistic life. The corporate celebration of the Eucharist symbolizes and brings about deeper relationships within the Christian community and between its members and God. The words of the Lord are spoken over the bread and cup according to his command. His death and resurrection are proclaimed and experienced by the community and every worshipper is caught up in this sacramental experience. This includes those who are present but, for a variety of reasons, do not receive Holy Communion. It is our duty and responsibility to find ways of including them fully in the worship. The Constitution of the Sacred Liturgy of the Second Vatican Council reminds priests that: 'It is their duty [also] to ensure that the faithful take part knowingly, actively and fruitfully.'[2] It also encourages them to take into account 'the age and condition of their people'.[3]

Although there will be a variety of spiritual experience and different levels of understanding within any congregation, the Eucharist, as the characteristic communal celebration of the Christian Church, should also be a vehicle for evangelization. Yet in many churches the way we present the Eucharist often obscures the truths contained within it, rather than revealing them. We need to find ways of enabling the Eucharist's power to speak to people more clearly so that they can come to discern the signs of our communion with Christ and with one another. This book is built on the growing sense that it is right for all ages to worship together at the Eucharist in a Christian community, whatever its denomination or tradition.

The question of admission to Holy Communion is beyond the scope of this book. In the Roman Catholic Church, it is at an early age. In the Free Churches, it is usually during the late teens. In the Church of England, the recent report, *On the Way* has attempted to examine both the whole issue of Christian Initiation and nurture of children and the radically divergent views about the appropriate age and the relationship between Baptism, Confirmation and Holy Communion. We are not concerned here with addressing the issues surrounding this, but with exploring how we can work and worship creatively within whatever tradition and situation that we find ourselves.

Two basic principles

The following statements underlie all the practical suggestions offered:

1. A fully Christian life gathers together all the baptized into a community of prayer and praise. The celebration of the Eucharist is central to this Christian life and is the fullest sign of our communion with one another and with God. Thus a developing understanding of the Eucharist is an essential part of the Christian life.
2. A programme of all-age Eucharistic worship and teaching will aim to help those at various stages of spiritual growth to appreciate the liturgy at the level appropriate to them. It should provide material to stretch everyone and also allow space to all.

Applying these two principles will realize the vision of a Christian community in which people of all ages are fully integrated and valued. At the same time it will safeguard against the risk of patronizing over-simplification or a sense of marginalizing other groups of people when large numbers of children are present.

Chapter Two
Spirituality and worship

Spiritual development – then and now

In recent years much has been written and researched on the theme of spiritual development of children and adults. This has been led by the work of James Fowler[1] in the USA. His theories have been explored in a straightforward and accessible style in the Church of England's report on faith development and Christian education, *How Faith Grows*.[2] While it is not necessary to become an expert on the subject in order to plan or lead all-age worship, it is advisable to have some idea of different people's spiritual needs and how they can be helped to fulfil them.

Spiritual development used to be related solely to the rote learning of the basic truths of the Christian faith. According to the Book of Common Prayer, children had to memorize the answers to a few questions and be able to recite the Lord's Prayer, Creed and Ten Commandments before being presented to the bishop for Confirmation and being allowed to receive Holy Communion. This may have been considered a normal way of teaching in sixteenth-century England but few people would accept that rote learning without discussion or application is an appropriate teaching style for today.

Sadly, however, elements of this attitude still hold strong. Many adults are surprised if a young child makes a comment which shows understanding of the presence or nature of God and decide that it has happened by chance. One argument used against children receiving Holy Communion is that they will not understand what they are doing or its importance – tacitly assuming that adults fully understand this great mystery and only ever approach the altar in the correct frame of mind.

During the 1960s there was a tendency to swing to another extreme and, following the thinking of Piaget[3] and Goldman,[4] assume that a

6

child's religious understanding would automatically develop as he or she matured. The magical 'Father Christmas' image of God would gradually change into the concept of an invisible and intangible spirit. Experience has shown that this rarely happens and that, while children develop mentally and physically, their basic spirituality often remains static and is gradually stifled until being finally rejected as 'childish'.

Fortunately, recent work on faith development is beginning to make itself known and it is being accepted that our pilgrimage through this life is not one of an automatic increase of spiritual understanding as the years go by. Nor is it just a case of assimilating facts which are gradually built up like learning mathematics or a foreign language. Instead of the journey of spiritual development being like climbing a ladder, a better analogy might be a spiral staircase. As he ascends, the pilgrim returns again and again to the same position but at a different height and so at a slightly new vantage point. He returns to the same experience of God but learns something different every time. An apparently simple faith may be the result of lack of thought or years but it may also have been arrived at after years of searching and questioning. A young child and a sophisticated adult may be closer spiritually than one would expect, for children have a natural spirituality which is often evident from an early age.

Allowing spirituality to develop

Spiritual development will include times of questioning and doubt as well as understanding because it is bound up with the development and articulation of the emotions as well as intellectual knowledge. The age when children tend to lose their open belief in God coincides with their going through a latent emotional period. They become less clinging and affectionate to their mothers. They no longer help with jobs or do school work to please their parents or teachers. They start saying 'Why should I?' and start to get their own ideas and make their own decisions. The spontaneous, 'I love that man', uttered by three-year-old Megan as she coloured in a picture of the crucifixion needs to develop and grow or it will be replaced by embarrassment and cynicism in a few years time as she heads out of the church door in search of the lesser demands of a local Boot Fair.

Just as there may be a temptation to 'freeze' Megan's comment because it articulates our own silent emotion to which we have returned after years of growth and discovery, there can also be a temptation to laugh at or dismiss childish beliefs. Children's first religious ideas come from what adults say and do but often they make different sense of them with surprising results. God is the vicar in the sky.

Angels are big fairies. Prayer is asking God for something and is bound up with being good. We need to be aware that, according to age and imagination, our children may pick up very varied images and ideas from our Christian worship.

'I can feel Jesus here,' said Jane putting her hand on her chest. She had taken literally the hymn of the previous week, 'O come to my heart, Lord Jesus', evoking a certain amusement on the part of her Junior Church leader, but she had also taken a step towards finding God within herself rather than a bearded figure on a cloud, an understanding that needs to develop as she learns to grasp abstract concepts. Young children take things literally, so trying to explain imagery will lead to difficulty. If we try to unpack similes of, for example, the Holy Spirit descending like a dove, we will cause confusion and eventually boredom. 'Like a dove' will imply another bird and questioning whether there was really a bird there will invite an exasperated, 'But why did you say there was?'

This is not a demand for all teaching to be simplified to banality, however, or for every word of more than one syllable to be explained to the point of the destruction of all colour and imagery.

Signs and symbols are important because it is through them that we 'earth' many of our abstract concepts. The rainbow as a sign of God's covenant with every living creature and a lighted candle as a symbol of the risen Christ are two examples.

Robert Cole's research into childhood spirituality[5] shows that many children have a deep insight into religious belief which, far from being misplaced, is both illuminating and humbling. Many parents and teachers have had experience of this. Children are indeed sensitive vehicles of spirituality because their minds are so less cluttered with problems and distractions than those of adults.

Miki, the youngest daughter of Vietnamese boat people, had watched some of her friends receiving Holy Communion at her Church school's termly service and, on impulse, asked if she could do so too. When asked why, her reply was, 'I want to be near to Jesus'. One may wonder if, after the weeks of teaching and learning that followed, she had ever expressed her longing and understanding in any better words than that brief statement.

Worshipping together

Taking the hints of profound spirituality and sense of mystery and wonder which seem to be an intrinsic part of young children and comparing them with the questioning, rejection and testing out of adolescence, one can see why many adults relate more easily to the spirituality of young children than that of teenagers. Adult knowledge and experience can bring renewal of a sense of wonder and mystery. Emotional maturity gives the security to enjoy simple things at a new level. We have the perfect example of this in the parables of Jesus, stories which can be heard by all ages because of their basic simplicity and the different levels of meaning within them. These homely stories shed light on the nature of God and our relationship with him, for they are ways of illuminating the inexplicable.

This communication of truths and human response to God simultaneously but at different levels is the nub of all-age worship. Perhaps this is shown most vividly at the Eucharist with its rich interplay of words and actions, signs and symbols. Young people, especially those who are going through the pressures of school and growing up, need to know that they are part of a Christian community which is meeting for celebration rather than a performance of a grim duty designed for selected adults at which children are barely tolerated.

Our own childhood memories can give some clues.

I could only see wood. I had to kneel and couldn't see over the top of the pew. *Alan*

The hall smelt of dust. The man playing the piano had his mouth open all the time. The boys called him, 'Ole monkey face'. I liked the real church with stained glass windows and the organ. *Frances*

Adults worship God. Children are taught about him. *David*

These comments conjure up a vivid picture of exclusion. Alan could not see what was happening. We need to question whether kneeling is the best posture for prayer if the pews form a visual barrier. Frances longed for the beauty of worship but was consigned to a dreary hall and honky-tonk piano. David's perception was that only adults knew enough about God to have a relationship with him. If he was good and learned enough texts, he might pass the test to become a 'proper Christian' one day.

In contrast, happy childhood memories of church are of a special person, a feeling of being wanted and loved, or a sense of wonder – a lightened candle in a darkened chapel, the sound of organ and trumpets on Easter morning, the silent figures on medieval tombs, the smell of incense or flowers. Here are the ingredients to offer to our young people: belonging and beauty. Our surroundings, posture, music and movement need to take into account the physical and emotional needs of everyone present. We should not assume that making worship accessible for youngsters entails destroying all that is beautiful and lovely because it may be not fully appreciated or understood. These matters are discussed further in the chapters on using music, movement and visual aids.

People of all ages need to experience that God is great and wonderful; that worship is a joyful celebration which is bound up with everything that we do. It is a way of placing oneself in the presence of God at any time, place or situation, tragic or joyful. The changing pattern of life is mirrored in the cycle of the Church's year as it moves from fasting to feasting, penitence to praise, death to new life. Corporate worship is just one aspect of this. Just as a family meets together to celebrate a birthday with a special meal, Christians meet as a community to celebrate the death and resurrection of Jesus in the Eucharist.

Learning through the senses

We retain most of what we learn by doing, a certain amount by what we see, and least of all by just listening. It is unfortunate, therefore, that much of our formal teaching in worship consists of a monologue from a static pulpit. Dialogue, acting out or reading a story in parts, as has been done with the Passion for centuries, will be far more effective teaching, especially to those who have taken part. Acting of parables can be brought right into the present day with modern situations, language and dress rather than the perennial headgear of tea-towels and a script peppered with 'thou's. Even a formal talk can include questions and answers if planned carefully while still retaining the importance of proclaiming and preaching the Word.

Similarly, parts of the church can be used as teaching aids. Stained-glass windows, monuments and paintings can call to mind a piece of teaching for weeks or even years. Visual aids can also be helpful but it is important to remember the age of the people one is teaching. A five-year-old will hold a candle wide-eyed with the magic of it or be fascinated by the intricacies of a buttercup but, by the time the same child is ten, the candle will be used for singeing the service sheet and flowers will be trampled on or, at the least, discarded as soppy. Older children will be more affected by the needs of the world around them, by political and moral issues. A group of teenagers in a multi-ethnic urban parish were totally uninterested in the story of the Children of Israel crossing the Red Sea until it was related to a recording of Martin Luther King's famous 'I have a dream' speech which then led to excitement, discussion and questions.

Children cannot be conned!

We need our teaching to be genuine and relate to everyday life.

Children cannot be conned. They will spot insincerity a mile away. Their minds are sharper than ours so they will point out inconsistencies in our conversation and teaching of which we may have been unaware, so we must beware of making blanket statements which we later have to amend or retract. Teaching that anger is always wrong and that Jesus was sinless will provoke difficult questions when we have the gospel about Jesus chasing the money-changers out of the temple. A weak, 'He was right that time' will be met with a sideways look and overt lack of conviction. Similarly, some of the more lurid stories from the Old Testament need careful handling. A bright child is sure to question God's love for everyone when learning of his drowning of the Egyptians, not forgetting the horses. Our explanation of the theme for the day, teaching on the Gospel and our intercessions need to bear this in mind.

The whole person

Just as the teaching and learning situation involves the whole person, so it is with worship. Children as well as adults need to participate fully, whether by gestures and responses from the pew or as servers, singers or readers. Then they will not just *hear* the Gospel but explore it in the way that is appropriate for their ages, whether with craft, dialogue, drama or discussion. They will be able to pray *with* the community rather than be prayed *at* by adults. Music, movement and language will be designed to make the worship accessible while retaining a challenge to the intellect and aesthetic values of all present whatever their ages and spirituality. To achieve this takes sensitivity, time and planning.

Chapter Three
Organization and planning

Applying the principles

A programme of all-age eucharistic worship should be carefully thought through and planned on the basis of the principles introduced in Chapter One. In particular:

1. The programme should help people of all ages to develop an understanding of the Eucharist as an essential part of the Christian life.
2. It should provide material to help everyone present, whatever their level of maturity, to grow in spiritual understanding.

There will need to be regular reviews of aims and methods to ensure that the principles have not been forgotten and the presentation remains fresh. Detailed planning and preparation are required. A haphazard approach is likely to result in lost opportunities and eventual disillusionment while planning and hard work will be richly rewarded. In the early stages, it will be necessary to give a lot of time to discussion, planning and rehearsing for all but the simplest services. As time goes by, however, and groups of people get used to working together and using the various resources available, it is amazing how quickly one can prepare work of a high standard.

Planning must be inspired with idealism but also earthed to what can be done effectively in practice. Flexibility is the key. When a particular plan is found to be too ambitious it must be simplified. When an idea, tentatively started, has been a great success, then it can be built upon. There will always be trial and error, even in the most experienced all-age parish. Planners should not set their sights too low, however; after all, those presenting the liturgy should be stretched as well as those participating from within the congregation.

A parish all-age Eucharist exemplifies the *pilgrim people* model of

12

the Church in action and will have something of the feeling of an extended family about it. Children from babies to teenagers will be present but they are unlikely to form the majority of the congregation since other generations will be be represented. A common pattern is to hold a regular monthly Family Eucharist, perhaps with a parade of uniformed organizations and with the children present throughout the service. This is the particular kind of service under consideration in this chapter.

Organization

Leading the whole Liturgy of the Word as well as providing imaginative art-work and music is a major undertaking and, apart from stretching the resources of a small group to its limits, needs far more time than a couple of weekly meetings to prepare. If a service is to be quite elaborate it is advisable to involve a wide range of people of all ages and levels of church allegiance. This is better for social, educational and liturgical reasons as well as the practical one of avoiding landing a few people with a major burden.

It may be that a particular individual who does not usually come to church can be invited to take part because he or she can make a special contribution. A Junior Church leader was delighted to discover that a retired lifeboat man had moved into the village and he was pleased to talk about his work to the children as part of their exploration of the gospel story about Jesus quelling the storm. Many Scripture passages are about God working in people's everyday lives and so a person's job, hobby or experience that is related to a particular story can bring it into today's world in a startling and vivid way.

Co-ordination of various groups who have limited time and familiarity with the church is a major undertaking and this will often fall upon the shoulders of one of the clergy or lay ministers. This does not mean, however, that this person has to organize and lead every aspect of the service, especially if they do not think they have the particular talents that are needed. They should rather act as a link and adviser, perhaps giving just a brief introduction and commentary during the service. On the other hand, it is important that the president is seen to preside over the whole liturgy and not just say the Eucharistic Prayer. This is for the theological reason that the whole community celebrates the whole Eucharist together, each member exercising the ministry appropriate to his or her role.

There are three practical 'musts' for the planning of an all-age Eucharist or, indeed, any act of worship which involves several groups of people:

1.   Allow plenty of time. It is hopeless to ask the Young Mothers to make banners at a couple of days' notice, only to find that one of them is on holiday and two others are coping with sick children. Similarly, music and drama always need more time for rehearsal than most people think.

2.   Have a 'belt and braces' approach. No act of worship should rely on one or two people being there. Not only is it unhelpful for people to feel indispensable, but it diminishes the contribution of the faithful chorus who work hard at a project only to have it cancelled at the last minute because the prima donna has not turned up.

3.   Make lists of everything and circulate them. It is never sensible to carry all the information in your head. Apart from the whole scheme falling apart if you are taken ill, it saves you from, 'What am I supposed to be doing tomorrow?' being left on your answer phone by a piping treble, usually without a contact number or name.

A preparation sheet like the one set out opposite may be useful.

Never take understanding and communication for granted. Always thank everyone individually who has done something special. Do not forget the children. A duplicated note with the name added is easiest and is always appreciated.

Worship committees

One way to organize a complex liturgy is to set up a worship committee or less formal planning group. This is recommended strongly in *In Tune with Heaven*, the report of the Archbishops' Commission on Church Music.[1] It suggests that such a group is made up of 'certain ex officio members – the clergy, director of music, others with particular responsibilities in worship – and representatives of the PCC, the congregation and particular constituencies such as the youth group'. This is rather a vague list. 'Others' could be more closely defined as readers, servers and sidesmen. 'Representatives' should include anyone with particular skills in, for example, drama or craft. Any educational activity, whether the Junior Church, mid-week club or adult study group should certainly be represented. Involvement of this kind can help to monitor the effects of the worship across the whole community.

Planning timetable

If the parish plans to have an all-age Eucharist once a month, the

Family Eucharist ... (date)

Theme/Aim ....

Celebrant ....

Sidespeople ....

Servers organized by ....

Music organized and led by ....

Visual aids made by ....

OHP operated by ....

Readers: OT .... **Epistle** .... **Gospel** ....

Homily/drama led by ....

Names of actors, speakers, and parts ....

Costumes/props needed/provided by ....

Offertory organized by ....

Holy Communion administered by ....

CLEARING UP AFTERWARDS LED BY ....

committee should try to meet about a week after each one to plan the next. This is for three reasons:

1. Memories of mistakes and ideas for improvement are still fresh in peoples' minds.
2. It allows for information to be distributed on the next Sunday, giving a week for any replanning needed and then two weeks for groups to organize their contributions.
3. A feeling of pressure at the beginning is not nearly as bad as a lack of time at the end.

Some clergy are reluctant to form such a committee, believing that it will be a vehicle for creating a monthly mish-mash of everyone's favourite ideas, strung together with a few popular Bible stories and hymns. This is a reasonable fear but need never happen if the committee gets its priorities right. Meeting should include time to study the theological and liturgical reasons for the Eucharist taking the form that it does so that, as will be discussed in Chapter Four, it is not seen as a strait-jacket to be discarded, but a skeleton on which to build a body. There are numerous options and alternatives that may be taken according to the situation. Awareness of the evangelizing aspect of worship and the pastoral needs of the congregation are important and may range from using short bidding prayers instead of lengthy intercessions to providing a service booklet with brief directions and explanations. Only after all these aspects have been borne in mind is there room for personal preference.

A flexible framework

The word 'framework' offers a key to the assessment of exactly what should be said and done at a particular all-age Eucharist. Balancing the time available and the inclusion of interesting and exciting material such as a drama may demand the curtailing of non-essential sections normally used. There is always a danger of the service becoming longer than the normal Sunday Eucharist. This should be avoided because of the young children and occasional worshippers who will inevitably be present. A balance also needs to be kept between what is theologically and legally required in the celebration of the Eucharist, and what constitutes permissible variation or legal experimentation. In practice, all churches seem to allow more scope for variation than is officially permitted.

In the Roman Catholic Church, the *General Instruction on the Roman Missal* and the *Directory of Children's Masses* offer a theoretical background and detailed interpretation of what should and should not be done in adapting or modifying the liturgy. For Anglicans, *The Canons of the Church of England*, together with the rubrics or instructions that accompany each service (e.g. the Notes which accompany Rite A of *The Alternative Service Book*) provide a framework within which those planning the liturgy are to work. Some diocesan bishops in the Church of England have issued supplementary regulations interpreting the Canons and rubrics or giving permission for local variation, such as to vary the readings or to substitute alternative material (e.g. the short Profession of Faith from the Baptism Service in place of the Nicene Creed). Other dioceses allow the use of Eucharistic Prayers from other Anglican provinces or from the Roman Catholic *Eucharistic Prayers for Masses with Children*[2] which follow a responsorial form.

The Canons allow some scope for the presiding minister to introduce material on a one-off basis so long as the doctrine of the Church of England is not contradicted by act, word or omission. General Synod has recently revised the Canons that apply to non-eucharistic Family Services. Eucharistic Prayers for use with children are in preparation.

How far can we go? It is worth remembering that, in general, rubrics and instructions are there to support the aims of the liturgy, so we must ask whether or not any variation from them will simplify and enhance the appropriate worship. The challenge is to establish a good practice whereby the liturgy can be attractively presented and adapted for all-age Eucharists in ways that let them speak to a situation without modifying too far the regular pattern of common prayer.

The liturgical year

The changing pattern of the liturgical year is a gift that we often neglect. We all enjoy the passing of the year with its festivals and holidays, its seasons and moods. Much school work revolves around these themes, and celebrations like birthdays and Christmas are key parts of the young person's year. The Christian calendar offers an even richer background of changing moods and images. The expectancy of Advent can be sensed by the atmosphere and surroundings – an Advent wreath, purple vestments and particular music – as well as by direct teaching in discussion and sermons. A special atmosphere surrounds Christmas while the idea of 'giving up something' during Lent has surprisingly strong power to attract young people. With some thought, Holy Week, Easter, Pentecost and saints' days can be lifted to an equal place in young peoples' minds. For centuries, the cycle of the liturgical year has been a key teaching aid to put us in touch with the saving work of Christ. The revival of imaginative ceremonies, full of symbolism and movement as in *Lent, Holy Week and Easter*[3] and *The Promise of his Glory*[4] has tremendous all-age appeal. Ways in which suggestions and parts of liturgies featured there can be implemented are shown in Chapter Four.

When planning all-age Eucharists over the course of the year, it is important to observe a balance reflecting the liturgical seasons. So, if, for example, in Lent the theme was penitence, the teaching could include a major section on how to say sorry to God for our sins. Such inclusion might make it necessary to compensate by curtailing the intercessions. The balance can be redressed when the theme is God's word, healing or compassion. Prayer for the needs of God's people would then have a correspondingly high profile.

Certain elements of the liturgy are indispensable to the celebration of the Eucharist and it is vital that any variations, omissions or alterations are grounded on sound eucharistic theology and not just the desire for an effective presentation. Nevertheless, it is not necessary to present every aspect of the whole story at every service. We can plan to use the whole of the Church's Year to teach and celebrate the mysteries of our salvation.

Parishes vary in their degree of commitment to following a liturgical calender and lectionary. In planning for Family Eucharists, however, a lively appreciation of the Church's Year will be a great help, since the seasonal prayers and readings provided offer a ready-made and varied foundation on which a parish can build its teaching.

Lectionary or themes?

In the progress through the Church's Year, a basic choice has to be made between a *lectionary-based approach* or a *thematic approach*.

The *lectionary-based approach* will take its cue from the readings presented by the Church for that particular Sunday or Feast day and work along these lines:

- What are these readings saying to us?
- How can we present them in appropriate ways for the congregation with its different levels of understanding?
- Are any variations necessary?

Whichever lectionary is used by a parish, it is sometimes hard to give positive answers to these questions in the all-age context. A particular reading, for instance, from St Paul on standards of Christian morality, may not be of immediate application to seven-year-olds and may be hard to present to adults too. Sometimes a reading set is inappropriately long and it may be advisable only to read a portion of it. Worship leaders must always be open to the possibility of varying a reading if it is really necessary, however committed a parish is to following the lectionary.

This approach offers the challenge of evolving the best possible presentation of given material as well as ensuring that a wide range of Scripture is read and studied throughout the two or three-year cycles of the various lectionaries. A mental or written index of resources spotted or used over the years will help to produce the right illustrative material for the right occasion – from the imagination, the filing cabinet or the props box – as planning becomes more focused. For the most organized leaders, a card index with suggestions for each Sunday noted as they come to mind would be a simple way of collecting and finding ideas. Notes on materials used, their successes and, even more important, failures, would also be useful.

The *thematic approach* will start with an initial decision about the subject to be tackled. In the short-term the approach could be along these sorts of lines: 'We have some good material on caring for the homeless. Let's run a Family Eucharist on the theme of compassion.' Planning is important, however, to ensure that the balance referred to earlier is achieved. Questions similar to those listed above will be asked, but they will come in a different order:

● What do we intend to teach today?
● How can we present it in appropriate ways for the congregation with its different levels of understanding?
● Which Scripture readings will help to expound the point?

One possible shortcoming of this approach is a lack of continuity with worship on other Sundays if the eucharistic lectionary normally used on other weeks is frequently abandoned. There are also the twin dangers of 'bees in bonnets' and repetition of a few well-tried themes rather than the stretching of minds to grapple with new ones.

Thematic Eucharists are especially appropriate when the majority of the congregation are children, maybe meeting as a school or a class. Young children can find it difficult to find a common idea or message in the different styles and situations in the lectionary readings, so a theme to which we return frequently can emphasize a particular aspect of the teaching of Christ or an important idea in the Christian life. Giving and receiving presents could be an appropriate theme for Epiphany. Exploring the different kinds of families could lead to teaching on the Church as the family of God, and so on.

Whichever approach is used, some flexibility is needed to take account of special occasions and celebrations such as Harvest

Thanksgiving, St George's Day, All Saints-tide, Sea Sunday, One World Week, etc. Christian charities often produce excellent ready-made material with suggestions for all-age worship, music, visual aids and prayers. Some teaching schemes also contain ideas for all-age worship which can easily be adapted or used as a starting point when planning a Eucharist. Even the most energetic and creative parish priest will be grateful for a few ideas and change of style from another source every so often.

If the lectionary is being followed, the likelihood is that, even when the same Sunday in the Calendar is marked down for a Family Eucharist in succeeding years, the reading will vary according to the three-year cycle of the Roman or two-year cycle of the Anglican Lectionaries. Where the thematic approach is used, planning will have to take account of the need for variety in treating particular recurring themes so that, for example, Pentecost 1996 is not a straight repeat of Pentecost 1995.

The planning process will try to ensure a right balance between different styles of presentation. This balance does not have to be identical each time, but over the months should include everyone and provide material to stretch all. Stereotypes should not be taken for granted, for example, children may prefer some traditional hymns to modern ones. It is impossible to please everyone all the time in the style and content of presentation and perhaps this is an important lesson in itself. There must be mutual forbearance among God's people, just as in any other human community, for learning and under-standing to develop.

Chapter Four

Step by step through the Eucharist

In planning all-age Eucharists, the liturgy is often treated as a strait-jacket from which we must escape. A more positive view is to see it as a skeleton supporting a living body, giving strength and freedom of movement in an ordered way. All too often, leaders spend time either trying to decorate the liturgical structure too elaborately or attempting to hide it altogether. The previous chapter considered various approaches to the liturgy as a whole and found room for flexibility and innovation. This chapter explores the rich resources that the Eucharist provides for all ages to worship together and suggests ways for developing parts of the service.

Before we start

A brightly coloured notice in the porch of a Kent church welcomes everyone to their parish church and then adds, 'Please talk to God before Mass and to each other afterwards'. This is not a recipe for a tense silence and unwelcoming attitude but for an atmosphere of calm and peace. Most people lead busy and noisy lives so they need time and space to relax and prepare themselves to worship God. This is especially so for parents who have had to get a young family ready or for people who are attending an evening Eucharist after a day's work.

There are a few guidelines which will help to set this atmosphere. First, it is vital that sidesmen see themselves as the official 'welcomers' to strangers as they will inevitably be the first contact that anyone will make with the church family. They should be ready, with books laid out at least 20 minutes before the service. A smile and a quiet greeting is all that is needed for most people; visitors may need information about the best place to sit, whereabouts of loos, etc. Again, this can be given quietly and pleasantly, in fact there is neither time nor place for gossip if the sidesmen are to do their job properly.

21

If it is possible to have dim lighting, this is also relaxing and the sense of expectancy can be generated by switching on the brightest lights a few minutes before the service. In practice, however, this is very hard to do successfully as half light can present a gloomy picture more akin to a closing-down sale than the preparation for a celebration.

There will always be some movement before the service as the altar is laid, music set out, etc. If this is done in an orderly fashion with no rush or noise, it can be seen to be as much a part of the preparation to worship God as individual prayers.

Music is always one of the most powerful ways of setting an atmosphere. Even today, the organ voluntary is the most usual form of music, but there is also an opportunity to use instrumental music or taped music if musical resources are very low or a special atmosphere is required.

All-age services always include a wide variety of hymns, some of which may not be familiar to all the congregation. New music can be rehearsed in a 'warm up' before the service begins. The patience of some congregations can wear thin if they are expected to have a hymn practice every week, but, at all-age celebrations it has the added bonus of calming excessive chatter and fidgeting as well as focusing the mind towards the liturgy. It can end a couple of minutes before the service with a request for silent prayer, often with profound results.

The introductory rites

The Entrance and Greeting

The most familiar way to open a service is by singing an entrance song, hymn or chant for which everyone stands and joins in. This fosters a spirit of unity among the congregation and encourages full participation from the outset. A well-known lively hymn needs to be chosen, or a less well-known one can be practised in a 'warm-up' as suggested in the above section.

The priest may begin with an invocation of the Trinity with the people making the sign of the cross. It is worth mentioning this because there is value in the idea of 'signing in' to the worship and prayer. The president then greets the people and they respond. If a pew leaflet is used there will be no need to announce page numbers, juggling of books or anything else that will break into the flow of the liturgy and disrupt the worship. It might occasionally be appropriate to use a less formal greeting such as, 'Happy Easter, everyone!' though unfamiliarity can lead to an awkward silence from the congregation.

After the Greeting from the president, a brief introduction from him or another leader will be useful in that it sets the tone and introduces the theme of the service. It is possible for the Peace to be exchanged at this time and some parishes value its being placed at this point in the liturgy. If the theme for the day were, for example, 'Getting to know our neighbours in Christ', there would a good reason for making it part of the Greeting.

'Lord have mercy'

Increasing numbers of parishes are finding it appropriate for the penitential prayers to take place at the beginning of the Eucharist. Having greeted each other and been reminded of the particular purpose of the celebration, we then call to mind our sins as part of our preparation for worshipping God. As the full rite of Confession, prayer for forgiveness and Kyrie is rather long, it is a good idea at a Family Eucharist to telescope them into a responsorial penitential rite, shown as an alternative in *The Sunday Missal; a new edition*[1] and suggested in *The Promise of his Glory*[2] after a short introduction and silence for reflection. The sentences can highlight a particular aspect of God's forgiving love or the theme of the Eucharist, and everyone can join in the responses.

As with many other parts of the Eucharist, some congregations stand for the penitential rite while others kneel for this and all prayers. Whatever the usual practice, standing is generally the better posture in all-age worship; small children have a knack of disappearing under the pews and most youngsters cannot see what is going on from a kneeling position. If standing is adopted, toddlers can be lifted up or stand on the pew while older children can usually move into a position where they can see. It may be easiest to stand from the opening hymn through to the end of the Gloria and Collect and then sit for the readings rather than complicate the service with unnecessary and disruptive movement.

'We praise you for your glory'

The *Gloria in Excelsis* is one of our oldest Christian hymns, but, because of its length and changes of mood, the majority of musical settings are quite difficult to sing. There are, however, several simple versions which have strong, memorable melodies. They are either for full congregational singing or use the first sentence, 'Glory to God in the Highest', as a refrain for everyone while a small group of singers sing the main portion of the text.

However limited a parish's musical resources are, the worst option of all for an all-age service is to abandon the music and say the Gloria. It removes much of the celebratory mood and it is always much harder to say long sentences together than to sing them. Moreover, there is a danger of children feeling devalued if things of beauty such as music and vestments are removed from 'their' Eucharist and nothing is put in their place. The comment of young Frances in Chapter Two is typical of the reaction of most children who enjoy colour, music and action. If the young people cannot cope with the whole Gloria or it is felt to be too long, a simple doxology or the 'Peruvian Gloria' from *Hymns Old and New*[3] which can be sung with just a guitar and percussion or even unaccompanied could be substituted. Other versions are discussed in detail in Chapter Five.

The Liturgy of the Word

'This is the word of the Lord'

Scriptural readings should be *heard*. This may seem obvious but many parishes find it hard to achieve, even with a sound system. They must be read slowly and clearly and, if young people are to read, they must rehearse carefully *in situ*. Even so, the voice that can normally be heard through walls or two sets of double glazing often will shrink to a whisper at the lectern. Getting children to take part as readers at a Family Eucharist is not always possible and, in the case of some readings, not appropriate. A particular tone of voice may not do justice to the proclamation of God's word and, of course, using children exclusively is denying the all-age element of this kind of worship.

Readings should be *understood* as far as possible, which means that readers, preachers, dramatists and commentators must do their homework on them so that they convey the sense correctly, grounded in their own understanding. It is also worthwhile giving thought to which version or translation should be used.

The advantages and disadvantages of sticking to the lectionary were discussed in the previous chapter, but, once a decision is reached, flexibility may still be needed. How many readings should there be? The ASB readings are often lengthy so a reading may need to be shortened or even omitted. A gruesome passage from the Old Testament or an intricate Pauline argument on sexual morality may be better left aside for exposition on another occasion. Readings in the Roman lectionary are generally shorter, long Gospels being marked with an abbreviated version.

At an all-age Eucharist, we need to ask which is the best way to present these readings. There is scope in this kind of worship to foster a sense of drama by using a variety of voices, maybe with a hidden character using a microphone to portray the voice of God. *The Dramatised Bible*[4] is a useful and flexible resource. Dialogue can be brought to life and even some intense arguments from the epistles can take on a new meaning when the form of the argument comes out clearly in the presentation. Again, rehearsal is vital as even the most dramatic passages of Scripture can lose all their force when poorly read. Other ways of portraying readings include acting or miming the narrative, holding up cards with key words, using simple props, pictures on paper, overhead projection or slides.

Comment on the Scripture readings is also often appreciated and can become a running homily, that is a commentary explaining the reading rather than a formal sermon which is less appropriate in an all-age context. In certain cases, it may be appropriate to have a commentary going right through the Eucharist, linking various parts of it with the scriptural readings. This was the sort of service that the Millers attended in the Introduction to this book and examples are given in Chapter Ten. A short paragraph can provide background or context, highlight images or arguments, link the readings together, and guide the congregation about a point to be noted.

Another interesting approach, found in the *Columba Lectionary for Masses with Children*[5] and geared to the Roman lectionary is a 'pre-reading' sketch in which a modern interpretation of the Scripture is presented, followed by the reading itself.

'Sing praise to greet his word'

Responsorial Psalms and Acclamations have become the norm in many parishes. As with using a responsorial setting for the Gloria, they are a practical musical medium to use with a congregation of widely varying ages and backgrounds. Young people usually join in the brief refrains with enthusiasm and gusto, including those who are unable to read. In parishes with traditional choirs that are wedded to plain-song or Anglican chant and regard modern versions with suspicion, it may be better to have a hymn or song at this point. One can use a metrical version of the suggested psalm, for example, 'Praise my soul the King of heaven' for Psalm 103, a hymn to greet the Gospel, for example, 'Song of Welcome for the Word'[6] or one linked with the theme of the readings. It is both pastorally and musically more satis-factory to have a mixed congregation join in such songs than to have those who are unfamiliar with the mysteries of pointing and pauses struggle mutely for enlightenment in yet another book.

'This is the Gospel of the Lord'

Great care should be taken to present the reading of the Gospel in a way that makes clear its special status as an encounter with Christ, the Living Word. Traditional ceremonial such as a procession, with candles and incense where used, can help. The reading can still be combined with drama, perhaps with the narrator speaking from the lectern while the action unfolds near the chancel step. There is much scope here for teaching that Christ speaks directly to us through the Gospel.

The homily

The aim of the Homily or Sermon is to expound, interpret and teach. It should be specifically related to the readings for the day, rather than being an unrelated, if well-illustrated talk. Numerous books have been published on how to deal with this part of the liturgy giving ideas for talks suitable for congregations with all ages present.[7]

When the running commentary model has been used, there may be no need to give a separate homily as well, or it may only need to be a brief drawing together of points already discussed. To promote interaction and involvement, the speaker can include every member of the congregation through question and answer techniques. The key point in this is that the speaker must know what point he or she wishes to get across. When putting questions to the congregation, it is also useful to have anticipated some of the possible problem answers and to be prepared to take them on board during the talk.

'We believe in one God'

The profession of faith in the Creed should sum up our response to God's word as heard in the readings and sermon. In practice, however, it is often a 'damp squib', especially if it has been preceded by some colourful visual aids or drama. As with the Gloria, it can be more effective if it is sung rather than said, but its very length makes it difficult for people to join in whether said or sung unless there is a very strong lead. Bearing in mind that the congregation at a Eucharist of this type will include people who only come to church occasionally, as well as young children, it may be an idea to dispense with the full Creed altogether and replace it with the Affirmation of Faith from the Service of Baptism[8] as suggested in Chapter Three. Even the youngest children can learn to join in the responses with some vigour. There are also a few hymn versions which cover the main points of the Creed which could be used if it is felt that the Affirmation of

Faith is an inadequate substitute. A full but easy one is 'We believe in God almighty' by Francesca Leftley, from *Hymns Old and New*.

'Lord, hear our prayer'

A group of people or a particular organization can take responsibility for the intercessions, each person being given a petition to read. If you have a sound system, it is a good idea to let the intercessors move in a line along the chancel steps with the microphone placed in the centre, or to group them around the lectern. Having people speaking from their seats dotted around the church can pose difficulties as some positions will have better acoustics than others and it is not easy for those listening to adjust their hearing to different directions without warning.

The intercessions present a first class opportunity for a wide variety of people that attend a Family Eucharist to be involved. If a group are to lead the intercessions, the timing of silence and responses will also need careful practice. At first, groups should have someone to act as editor as well as offering suggestions for subjects. The most common danger is that petitions become too detailed and verbose. Fortunately, young people rarely fall into these traps and their prayers sound just as they ought to be – natural, straightforward and to the point.

A subject should rarely be vetoed as unsuitable because this can give the impression that God is not interested in for example the welfare of criminals or a little girl's dead gerbil. Children should be encouraged to write their own prayers rather than reading out an intercession that someone else has written in an unfamiliar vocabulary. There is further discussion on using groups as intercessors in Chapter Nine.

The Liturgy of the Sacrament

'The peace of the Lord be always with you'

In most parishes the exchanging of the Peace has established itself as a regular feature, but, in those where there is embarrassment or resistance, the all-age Eucharist may prove a helpful opportunity to show how natural it can be. Children's faces when they greet each other with a sign of peace indicate how much this part of the liturgy means to them. It might be worth challenging parishioners to ask themselves whether they know the names of the young people with whom they share the Peace. The Peace may be exchanged at other points: as part of the Greeting (see above) or between the Lord's Prayer and receiving of Holy Communion.

The Offertory

After a long and often largely static period, the congregation is likely now to either stand or sit to sing a hymn. On Sundays when the children have had their own Liturgy of the Word, this is usually the time when they join the rest of the congregation. People of all ages should be encouraged to take their part in any procession of the bread and wine or of the Offertory up to the chancel step. If the children have worked on a particular topic recently and produced something like a collage, it would be appropriate for them to present this as a token of their work. As this is a time in the service when there is plenty going on at the altar, it is a good idea to encourage the children to watch the action. It would be worthwhile occasionally to replace the Offertory hymn with a chant or song that can be sung from memory so that the congregation can watch the action and join in the prayers and spirit of the Offertory at the appropriate moments.

The Eucharistic Prayer

Different traditions in the Christian Church give different weight to the Eucharistic Prayer and have different ways of explaining its significance. All agree that it holds a position of crucial importance in the celebration of the Eucharist as it presents the Lord's words and actions at the Last Supper and makes a memorial of his death and resurrection until he comes again.

Sadly, through poor presentation and balance, the Eucharistic Prayer can often seem a terrible anticlimax. Many parishes produce imaginative and involving presentations of readings, talks, intercessions, and Offertory with music, action, colour and style. Then follows a clerical monologue, often lacking any style at all, when the congregation may become restless and inattentive, distracted and irreverent.

There is no simple way ahead in meeting the challenge of raising the level of congregational devotion and involvement during the Eucharistic Prayer. First and foremost, it is vital to make the congregation aware that the Eucharistic Prayer is the Church's Prayer, articulated by the priest on behalf of the whole assembly, but *prayed by everyone*.

The key problem in constructing Eucharistic Prayers or presenting them at all-age worship is finding simplicity of expression without over-simplification of content. The Roman Catholic Church has approved three Eucharistic Prayers for use at Masses with children which use simpler language with short phrases, interspersed with congregational acclamations, preferably sung. As stated in Chapter Three, some Anglican dioceses have authorized use of these, while 'official' ones are in preparation. Ironically, the Roman Catholic Prayers for Masses with Children tend to be longer than the usual Eucharistic Prayers but they do have added involvement.

A particular area for experiment and development is that of the congregational response during the Eucharistic Prayer, already provided for in part by the introductory dialogue, the Holy, Holy, Holy Lord, the Memorial Acclamation and the Amen at the end of the Prayer. It is perfectly feasible to introduce acclamations into any Eucharistic Prayer.

The texts all refer to certain actions performed by the Lord at the Last Supper, and it helps children if they can see the president performing clear actions in taking the bread and wine during the narrative of institution – the audio-visual heart of the prayer. They may feel more intimately associated with the saving work of Christ if a group of them are allowed to stand around the altar during the Eucharistic Prayer on some occasions. As already pointed out in considering posture at the Penitential Rite, even if the people generally kneel during part of the Eucharistic Prayer, it may be better for the smallest children to stand so that they can see, rather than kneel and lose the line of sight. Although this could pose a threat of distraction for others, in practice, most children seem to be quite still and attentive, sensing the atmosphere of devotion that the Prayer demands.

Our Father

As well as being a moment when everyone can join in, children often respond well to an invitation to extend their arms, as the president may be doing, in the ancient *orans* position – standing with arms pointing towards heaven, palms opened. A variation of this is for each person to join hands with his or her neighbour during the prayer or for everyone to join hands and hold their arms up. These kinds of gestures, or the more elaborate ones suggested in Chapter Eight on movement and dance, give a sense of reality to the description of the Lord's Prayer as the 'family prayer' of Christians. It is also an opportunity to help all members of the congregation to gain a powerful image of their unity in Christ and of their role as a praying people.

Which version?

In most denominations and in schools, the traditional form, 'Our Father, who art in heaven' is the version most likely to be used, though the ASB version, 'Our Father in Heaven' may be used in some Church of England Schools. The traditional version tends to be the one known by occasional visitors in that it is commonly used at weddings and funerals as well as in Roman Catholic and Free Churches. It is up to parishes to decide which version they will use, taking all these considerations into account. If both the traditional and ASB versions are used at different times, it is probably more important to have consistency across the local Church school, the Junior Church and the Family Service than to use the same version at the Eucharist every week.

During and after Holy Communion

This section is not a discussion on the thorny subjects of Communion before Confirmation or at what age children should be allowed to receive Holy Communion. It is an attempt to look at ways of using whatever situation is found in a church or community, bearing in mind that communicant status has little to do with age in a society where the majority of people are not members of a church.

The variety of people at an all-age Eucharist is enormous, ranging from the regular communicants, through the children who are used to receiving a blessing at the altar each Sunday, to people of all ages who have no particular church affiliation or the family of a child who is taking a special part. This is highlighted when the young children from a uniformed organization come to the altar together and some of them, not necessarily the oldest, receive Holy Communion while the others, including maybe the leader, receive a blessing. On the other hand, to see adults as well as the children receiving a blessing does a great deal to alleviate the impression that Holy Communion is for adults only.

Children usually join in the procession to the altar with enthusiasm and this is further heightened if they are able to sing a song which sets the atmosphere at the same time. Some of the *ostinati* from Taizé or simple hymns like, 'Abba, Father' and 'Father, we love you' from *Mission Praise*[9] immediately spring to mind.

Even if there is a large number of children, they should all be invited forward for a blessing. The practice in a few parishes and schools of choosing representatives of classes or organizations to receive a blessing is divisive and a denial of God's generosity to *all* of his people. The atmosphere usually calms the liveliest youngster and the risk of a bit of wriggling is far less than that of rejection, which could have far-reaching effects. Many a child has gone to the altar sullenly and walked away smiling while rubbing the top of his head to see if it is different in any way! Similarly, the procession to the altar should follow the normal order, with no group singled out because of its age or status.

If there is to be a period of silent reflection after Communion, a few words of commentary can help everyone to direct their thoughts and focus their attention on the meaning of the Eucharist. Meditative instrumental, vocal or taped music can also be used to enrich the atmosphere at this point.

In some parishes, it is a practice to follow Communion immediately with a thanksgiving hymn. The alternative is to sum up our thanks in the Postcommunion prayer which leads straight into the Blessing and Dismissal. This saves a lot of movement in churches where it is customary to kneel for the Blessing. Then the congregation can rise to sing a thanksgiving hymn which also acts as a recessional. The Eucharist thus ends with everyone standing and singing together in a joyful frame of mind.

Chapter Five

Music

An expression of unity

The comments most frequently heard after any act of worship concern the music. 'We sang my favourite carol' or 'I didn't know the hymns' are far stronger criteria of a 'good' service for occasional visitors to a church than the most stirring sermons or profound prayers. The Miller family, featured in the Introduction to this book, recognized the opening hymn from a television programme and Stephen Miller remembered the tune for the Lord's Prayer from his own childhood. Learning a chant from *Music from Taizé*[1] before the service and singing it during Communion, also helped to make the whole family feel involved and welcome.

Music is perhaps the strongest way there is of expressing a corporate feeling. Eighty thousand fans singing 'Abide with me' at a cup final can be just as emotional a moment as seeing the winning goal scored. So it is with music in worship. The Eucharist is a shared activity of people gathered together and this is best portrayed by corporate singing because the 'one voice' heard is that of the community expressing its unity in Christ and with each other. The Miller family, though strangers to St Mary's, gained a sense of belonging by being able to join in some of the music and thereby feel that they contributed actively to the worship.

A vehicle of emotion

As well as the corporate feeling that springs from singing, music portrays and affects emotions far more deeply than speech so, through it, the whole range of human life can be expressed and offered to God. As it is also the most abstract of arts, having to be constantly recreated, it can also express the mystery and intangibility of God.

Music is a gift from God to be used to his glory. In return God gives back a glimpse of himself to the worshipper.

This does not mean that music in worship has be 'difficult' or performed by experts. Psalm 23, 'The Lord is my Shepherd', can convey absolute trust in God through all the joys and difficulties of life in a variety of simple versions and tunes. Intoning the Eucharistic Prayer over quiet moving chords, as practised at Lourdes, can produce a great sense of mystery and awe if done with sensitivity. The pure tone of a flute solo can lead to silent prayer, while a stirring accompaniment like Vaughan Williams' setting of 'All people that on earth do dwell' can take a congregation from grandeur, through tranquillity to triumphant joy in just five short verses.

We celebrate the Lord's death and resurrection when we meet for the Eucharist and most celebrations include music as our basic expression of joy. This being so, music must be planned as an integral part of the worship, not just a few hymns added at the last minute, maybe by someone who has had no connection with preparing the rest of the service. It is not a case of, 'We had better have a popular hymn for the children here' but, 'What style of music will add to this part of the liturgy? Should it be sung or played and how long should it last? What text and mood will give the appropriate emphasis?' and so on.

Infinite variety

Hymns and versions of the Psalms have been the mainstay of Anglican and Free Church worship since the Reformation, but the explosion of new congregational music during the last thirty years allows infinite variety that can be used with great advantage in all-age worship. Many new hymns are designed for unison singing with guitar, piano or keyboard accompaniment, rather than for four-part choir and organ. There has been a revival of responsorial and antiphonal forms as used in the worship of the early Church, and varied instrumental melodies are used to enhance simple chants like those from Taizé. Music from other religious centres such as Iona[2] and Lourdes[3] add straightforward hymns and songs, many with a folk-like idiom. Sadly, many parishes have either completely ignored the opportunities offered by these new styles or have embraced them with such gusto that traditional hymn books containing much that is of lasting value are totally excluded.

A middle path is best and it is possible for an all-age Eucharist to have all-age music, ranging from ninth-century plainsong, through various styles of hymns to a number composed only last week. Every need and music taste can be catered for without having a hotch-potch of styles which grate against each other if the fundamental criterion of fitting music to the liturgy rather than seeing the music as an end in itself is adhered to.

Music in the Eucharist falls into four basic uses:

1. to provide an atmosphere for worship with instrumental voluntaries or as a background to speech or chant;
2. to accompany movement or other action such as a procession or reception of Holy Communion;
3. to set a text such as the Gloria or the Sanctus;
4. to be an entity in itself such as a hymn or a psalm.

Hymns and songs

To promote active participation, hymns should be familiar and also singable by everyone. This does not mean a reduction to a few favourite numbers which are repeated on every possible occasion. Even the best music becomes dull and tedious after a while. Neither does it mean using only hymns that are sung at the local primary school or those with bouncy rhythms that were written in the last ten years. As stated in the comments on spirituality in Chapter 2, there is no need to reduce everything to the most trite and banal in an attempt to provide instant understanding. Children will soon pick up a strong traditional hymn if the rest of the congregation sing it well and new material can always be learned during a previous week's teaching session if the leaders have the music list in advance. This will add to their repertoire of hymns that are deservedly part of our heritage.

However, it is a good idea to be aware of what is being sung in schools today. Most primary schools use either the BBC's books, *Come and Praise* 1 and 2[4] or the many books in the *Someone's singing, Lord* series, published by A & C Black.[5] Although designed for assemblies, they all contain hymns and songs which are suitable for all-age Eucharistic worship and can give the children a chance to lead the adults. 'Water of Life' and 'I will bring to you' from *Come and Praise* 1 are good examples.

If this is truly all-age worship there would be no need to put in a song especially for the children. Doing so would be exlcusive in itself and thus damage the concept of the worship being that of the whole people of God together. It will also tend to cause a break in the flow of the liturgy. There may be an occasion when it is appropriate to sing, 'If I were a butterfly' or a similar song but it should not happen every week. This does not mean, however, that a group of children cannot lead everyone's worship at an all-age service by offering music on their own in the same way as an adult choir might sing a Communion anthem.

New music can be introduced with a congregational practice about five minutes before the service is due to begin as suggested in Chapter Four. It is never a good idea to have a general rehearsal after the service or immediately before the music is performed. Carefully managed, a practice can be a part of greeting the congregation and a practical way of helping people to join in. It is always best to keep the rehearsal short and to be encouraging. Finishing with thanks and a smile is more likely to lead to a good performance after a feeble rehearsal than a comment like, 'Well, that was not much good, but it will have to do because the priest is looking at his watch.' The organized sound of a structured rehearsal can also be a good way of leading into a positive silence for a few minutes before the service.

Settings

In spite of the increase in congregational participation, there have been very few settings of the Eucharist written that are truly designed for congregational singing. 'Unison' does not always mean simple and many unison settings have their interest in exciting but very complex organ parts which demand a strong band of experienced singers to hold the melody line. Others are written for a choir with a congregational part that may not be suitable for encouraging the participation that is a hall-mark of an all-age Eucharist. There is a vast choice of settings for the church with a strong choir and large congregation, but little to help the small parish with few musical resources. Fortunately, this is beginning to change and several composers have written settings in the folk idiom for the ICEL text which can be used by both the Roman Catholic Church and the Church of England, so there is more choice available than is immediately apparent.

Of settings for congregation alone, Dom Gregory Murray's *New People's Mass*[6] is very easy to pick up (the writer used it regularly in an inner-city primary school) and both Paul Inwood and Christopher Walker have written several simple but attractive Masses for congregational singing. Examples of these will be found in *Music for the Mass*.[7] For an even simpler option from the same book, the *Responsorial Mass* by David Whitehead and Derek Fry has the full text sung by a soloist or small group with everyone singing sections as a refrain.

Written in a more Anglican style, Tambling's 'Holy Trinity Service' from *Five more Parish Settings*[8] is bright and straightforward and Martin How's *Music for the Parish Communion*[9] follows the responsorial form. In parishes where there is an established choir this also allows for the contrast between small and large groups of singers as well as maintaining the choir's role of leading the singing in a service which will usually have simple, congregational music.

Psalms and chants

Responsorial psalms provide another interesting contrast between a soloist, singing group and main congregation. There is no need for a choir, or even an accompaniment; a singer with a clear voice can lead from a lectern or even his or her place. The *Responsorial Psalter*[10] provides similar material for use with the Roman lectionary and *Psalms for the Eucharist*[11] contains arrangements of psalms to go with the ASB lectionary. Chants from *Music from Taizé* which are usually verses from Scripture are easily learned and can be sung from memory, either repeated several times or interspersed with solo verses.

Instrumental music

Every liturgy needs space for contemplative prayer. Instrumental music to set the mood of the liturgy and solo or choral singing commenting on some aspect of it can be offered by those with such talents but prayed by everyone. Instrumental music has traditionally been used for voluntaries and for 'filling in' but pieces can also be played during the Offertory or as an aid to meditation.

Many young people are highly skilled musicians and can make a valuable contribution to worship in this way. Some churches have their own folk group or a few instrumentalists who can perform upon occasions. If the local school has an orchestra, guitar or recorder group it could be invited occasionally to provide the music. This has an evangelistic dimension too. Many young people have come to a church service for the first time as part of a visiting music group and have returned as part of the congregation, youth club or choir. All of this requires preparation but young people are usually happy to help make music if they are given time to practise it. Music in schools today stresses composition as well as performance, so there may be a youngster who will write a hymn tune or instrumental piece for the parish as part of his or her GCSE course work.

If your parish has a dearth of musicians, there is no need to give up. Taped music can still provide suitable background music and one confident singer can lead a whole congregation with great effect and more success than a poor accompanist. A melody line can be played on a keyboard or even a solo recorder. It is worth remembering that, for the majority of the Church's history, singing was a single unaccompanied melody. While the people of God have voices, they can sing to his praise.

Chapter Six

Drama

Principles

An argument once took place between two clergy, one of whom alleged that the other presented the Eucharist in an over-dramatic way. The other replied, 'But the Eucharist *is* a drama.'

When considering drama within the Eucharist, the first principle is that nothing should upstage the words and actions of the Lord over the bread and cup. If the significance of the Eucharist is diminished in any way by a piece of drama, then this drama is out of perspective.

The second principle is that we should only do what we can do worthily. A short, well prepared mime or sketch with a simple message will have a far more lasting effect on the congregation than an elaborate, badly produced play, however brilliant the script or profound the teaching it contains. We need to set our sights sensibly and avoid the temptation to include too much in content or elaborate effects and costumes.

The third principle is that everything should be seen and heard. In a traditional church building this may be hard to achieve but it is destructive of the congregation's sense of unity if a sketch is heard and seen only by the select few at the front of the nave. An easy way around this is not to restrict the action to the chancel step, but to use the whole church – the nave, side aisles, pillars and pews.

The fourth principle is that such dramatic episodes, like those performed in the theatre, must involve the hearts and minds of the members of the congregation if they are to be successful.

Basic types of drama for all-age Eucharists

Sometimes a professionally written play performed in part or in whole, may carry great teaching opportunities. *Murder in the Cathedral* by

T. S. Eliot[1] or a sketch from *The Little Flowers of Saint Francis*[2] are two well-known examples. These may be performed with props and simple scenery, and can usually speak for themselves without being diminished by subsequent interpretation.

Simple sketches may be useful aids to understanding the readings, particularly if they are given beforehand and present the biblical idea in contemporary idiom. *The Columba Lectionary for Masses with Children*[3] presents such sketches, geared to the readings of the Roman lectionary. Young people may, with appropriate guidance, be able to prepare such sketches after discussion of the meaning of the reading in a group beforehand.

Often it is possible for whole readings to be acted out. *The Dramatised Bible*[4] sets the majority of the Scriptures for reading by different voices. *Sketches from Scripture* and *Acts for Apostles*[5] include short sketches presenting the readings in modern idiom which can be performed by a group from about ten years old with very little rehearsal. Moving away from straight biblical plays, older children and adults may enjoy performing the light-hearted but thought-provoking dialogues from the Iona Community, *Eh ... Jesus ... Yes, Peter ...?*[6] which are based on the gospels but are a series of imaginary conversations between Jesus and an eager, but sometimes obtuse disciple.

Mime is another useful vehicle where planning requires a sense of worship more than drama-school training. It can be used continuously while the text is narrated by one or many voices, or it can be developed as a set of tableaux. Where several people are involved, adequate rehearsal is needed, not least so that those involved can make their entrances smartly and sustain the movement of the reading or sketch. Mime also needs rehearsal as the actors need to memorize their cues for action. When a script is being written it saves enormous trouble and a lot of time if the words describe what the person miming is actually doing.

'Jesus knelt down and prayed; he lifted up his hands and looked up to heaven and said, "Father, if it is possible, let this cup of suffering pass."' Such a technique is not as obvious to the congregation as it seems and makes mime much more successful because it ensures that words and images coincide. It is a good idea to go through a mime without the script being read at some point in rehearsal. This is in order to make sure that the gestures and movements are clear in themselves.

Gestures

Simplicity is the keynote in planning movement. Gestures should be expansive and generous, not cramped and mean. It is important for actors to feel natural with them, but this is not always easy when working with children. An embrace between Mary and Joseph will cause chronic embarrassment for ten-year-old actors who are unwilling to come near one another, but can bring a rehearsal to a halt when a fifteen-year-old couple cannot be disentangled!

One of the most dramatic points in a Good Friday Passion Play is when Jesus is nailed to the cross. The effect of a loud bang against wood accompanied by Jesus's hand being flung back against the cross sounds little enough on paper but the effect is electrifying for both adults and children.

Dramatic action involving everyone

In the course of the Church's year there are a number of occasions when the whole congregation can be drawn into a dramatic action. A Palm Sunday procession, preferably starting away from the church and processing to it to re-enact Jesus's entry into Jerusalem rather than a walk around the church for no apparent reason gives everyone a chance to move, sing or shout and wave palm branches. Real greenery can be used or the children can make palm trees by painting and cutting rolled up newspaper. Generally speaking, the larger the branches, the more joyful the action! Another event is a procession with candles in a darkened church to celebrate the 'Light to lighten the Gentiles' on 2 February, the Presentation of the Lord. Many other ideas can be found in *The Promise of his Glory*[7] and *Lent, Holy Week and Easter*.[8]

The role of the director

It is not necessary to have drama-school training to direct a highly successful piece of drama during a liturgy. Anyone who has taken part in school or amateur dramatics should have picked up sufficient tips to be able to plan and carry through a good piece of acting or mime and will become more confident with experience. All that is required is careful planning. The script must be read through before rehearsal to ensure that it will work in the particular building and with the people who are available. It is also important to check that everyone who wants to take part will be present on Sunday, preferably with a note or call to the home. Youngsters' memories can be remarkably selective when something more exciting turns up at the last minute.

If young people or, indeed, people of any age, are to be involved in drama successfully, they should regularly have some kind of dramatic activities in their Junior Church or Youth club. These can range from simple games to miming or acting with masks and are always popular. Sadly, this aspect of teaching and learning is often left out until mid-November when children and adults are suddenly expected to acquire new skills and techniques to present a full-scale Nativity play to the entire congregation. A number of books of games and activities are available.[9]

A church is not usually an easy building for producing drama so resources must be used to bring out their strengths; a large Victorian pulpit can block or cramp badly-positioned action, but it can also serve as a boat, a home for the angelic host or even a tomb. Adaptations may need to be made at various stages and these should always be noted by everyone involved, whether acting, providing costumes and props or just playing the final music. It is often a good idea to make characters responsible for providing their own props which can be very simple; a walking stick can indicate that a person is old or very sick, a bread basket passed around a group will give the impression of people sharing a meal, and hats can be used to imply an actor's character if full costumes are not available.

During rehearsal, the drama should be looked at from the congregation's point of view. This can be taken literally by having someone seated at the back of the church or moving around it during rehearsals to check for audibility and visual effect, but it also applies to the congregation as recipients of the drama as part of the Ministry of the Word. The director and worship leaders need to ask questions constantly:

- Will this play illustrate the gospel more vividly?
- Will this sketch give everyone, whether young or old, food for thought?
- Will its message be clear enough to help each person to grow a little in his or her Christian life ... or will it just be a facile entertainment to give the youth club a feeling of belonging?

Good drama can add a powerful extra dimension to any act of worship. It is a medium in which anyone, whatever their age or level of skill, can take part in some way. It will be taken notice of because it is the kind of audio-visual communication from which people in our generation acquire most of their information. Actions speak louder than words.

Chapter Seven

Visual aids

The church building

Worship often takes place within a wonderful visual aid which is frequently neglected or even ignored – the church itself. Many parishes only see their church as an expensive and restricting burden. We need to look at it positively and ask, 'How can we make the best use of it to enhance our worship?'

An all-age Eucharist works much more naturally with a free-standing altar near to the congregation with the president facing the people and seen clearly by them, than with a far distant ceremony at the east end of the church, maybe almost masked by a wrought iron screen. Complete reordering of a church with ancient or elaborate screens and chancels is hardly possible, and might not be thought desirable, but many parishes solve the problem by having a movable altar in a central position for the Family Eucharist, reverting to the older pattern for other Sundays. The church building will mean more if it is used to its full potential through light, sound, colour movement and appreciation of the function of each of its component parts.

Among the features of the worship environment which can be built upon for all-age Eucharistic worship and teaching are:

- the shape, size and feel of the building
- stained-glass or other decorative windows
- pictures, icons or statues
- the font, altar, pulpit and other furnishings
- candles and lighting
- liturgical colours

Some churches have the instant visual appeal of extraordinary beauty which can reduce even the most sceptic agnostic to silence. The average church may not be this attractive, but a sense of God's pres-

42

ence is often created by the architecture, decorations and furnishings of a simple parish church, whether medieval or modern.

Most of us find that we continually discover something new about an environment which seems so familiar to us. We notice a new view on a habitual walk, or a pattern created by the sunlight shining through a dusty window. This process of discovery and learning can be applied easily to a church building.

Windows, pictures and carvings

The report, *All God's Children?*[1] mentioned cathedrals as an evangelistic resource but this can be equally true of the parish church, both for visitors and for the regular congregation. Occasional visits by schools, colleges or other groups of adults as well as children provide an opportunity to use the building in this way. Stained-glass windows and murals taught the faith to generations of people who could not read and did not possess Bibles. In an age where people are unwilling to read and the Bible lies untouched on most book-shelves, images are once again needed as we are subjected more and more to the impact of television and videos. A Fun Day, a talk, or a whole Eucharist could be built on the history behind the stained-glass windows or the message told by them, whether they be Victorian or modern, abstract or full of traditional images.

The presence of icons, statues or religious pictures varies with traditions of churchmanship. Those who have visited or worshipped in an Eastern Orthodox Church will be familiar with the way that countless saints are represented: Jesus and Mary are to be found on the iconostasis (screen) with the patron saint of the parish and the apostles, together with the whole heavenly host. These create an awareness that the Christian family embraces earth and heaven and extends through time and space: '... with angels and archangels and the whole company of heaven ...' The sense of being part of this family is extremely powerful.

The Western church has always been more restrained in its use of images, but surviving or restored painted medieval screens, ceilings and sometimes walls, create a similar effect. Some churches will have a statue of Mary with the infant Jesus or of a patron saint. In both Western and Eastern traditions the holy men and women of God are often portrayed in art with symbolic objects relating to their story: St Peter with keys which remind us of Jesus's words, 'I give you the keys of the kingdom of heaven' and St Paul with the sword of his execution are well-known examples. Where images of saints themselves are not available or favoured, these emblems can sometimes be found on banners or embroidered on hassocks and be valuable for all-age worship and learning. *Saints, Signs and Symbols*[2] is a useful teaching and artistic aid for this work.

Furnishings

The most obvious items of furniture in many churches are rows of pews or chairs. These are often regarded as a restrictive nuisance, especially if they are fixed, but with imagination, they can be used positively in drama. They can become houses in Bethlehem for a nativity play, as used in *The Christmas Star* by Malcolm Williamson,[3] or they can become a grandstand for children who can be invited to stand on them to see a baptism or drama more clearly. One church portrayed Gladys Aylward's missionary travels across China by using them as mountains to be climbed over.

A visit to a cathedral or ancient basilica with the nave cleared of chairs, however, refocuses attention on the altar, font and pulpit. In many churches the font is found near the entrance, an ancient tradition favoured once again by experts on church design and layout. Increasingly, the altar is to be found in the midst of the people so that the president can face them and the impression of the faithful gathered around the Lord's table can be promoted. Modern liturgical commentators emphasize that the altar should not be cluttered to the point of detracting from its purpose. In one parish, the children were asked to draw a picture of the altar and what went on it. In three quarters of the drawings the vicar's glasses were in pride of place. Only a few had shown the bread and wine.

Some churches now arrange for the readings and sermon to be given from one place, the 'ambo' of the ancient basilicas, and the pulpit or lectern thus forms a single focus for the Ministry of the Word. Stations of the Cross, an open Bible or a prayer request board all offer different opportunities for teaching.

Candles and other lighting

A candle reminds us that Jesus is 'the light of the world'. Lighting a candle is a gesture that is being increasingly rediscovered across all traditions as an aid to prayer, an expression of longing for God or a desire for someone's well-being that cannot be expressed in words. Most cathedrals have candles flickering all day long in a place of prayer or pilgrimage. In some parishes, candles are used on the Feast of the Presentation of the Lord (see Chapter Six) or at the Easter Vigil service of Light on Holy Saturday. The visual and spiritual appeal of the living flame of a candle should not be underestimated.

The dreariest or least architecturally appealing church can be brought to life by the careful use of light. Even where a new lighting system is financially out of the question, a well-placed and carefully aimed domestic spotlight can have a transforming effect, creating focus, contrast and depth. Lights can also be dimmed and raised at various points during a service to good effect.

First Impressions

Every service held in church has a visual impact. We need to be acutely aware of this and to ask what people will make of what they see in church. Stories are often told about comments made by the clergy, supposedly as quiet asides, which have been broadcast accidentally through the sound system. The *visual* indiscretions in worship are often even more embarrassing. Everyone involved in leading worship needs to sit down from time to time to think afresh about what they do, the way they do it, and what, in fact, these actions are communicating. The way we walk, stand and read convey our commitment and sincerity or lack of them. Processions and movement require timing and rehearsal. Readers should be ready to speak and stand still and upright. Musicians should look attentive during all the service, not just the musical bits. Robes and altar linen should be clean and crisp. The president should remember that he is always on view. Young people will notice even the smallest slips and rejoice in them or puzzle over their significance.

It is often the visual images that last longest – the sight of hundreds of pilgrims in a procession at night carrying lighted candles, the simplicity of a child kneeling before a small doll in a Nativity Play, the starkness of the cross on Good Friday. Often worship planners and leaders work needlessly hard and overburden worship with words when a visual image that is already in place would convey the message far more simply and effectively.

Artwork

The fullest all-age expression of art in church would be a complete redecoration project in which everyone played their part. This is rarely possible but there is much potential in decorating the building with banners and posters, making frontals for the altar and falls for the lectern and pulpit. An early decision has to be made whether perfection or involvement is the primary aim in preparing artwork. A frontal made by a group of youngsters for Harvest Thanksgiving will look and say something different from one made by the Women's Fellowship.

An elaborate banner needs to be made by experts. A much simpler design will look none the worse for having been assembled by a mixed group. Felt, glue and staples can often achieve as good an effect as intricate embroidery. In planning banners or hangings, it is important to establish the following criteria:

- Where is the banner going to hang? This will influence size and shape as well as the boldness of design. The tendency is to make banners too small, detailed and subtle.
- How will it be hung? Being propped up in a corner is not the only answer. Banners can be hung from hooks against the wall at either side of the east window with great effect. They can also be suspended from bars in a similar way to flags in a military chapel. If either of these places are used and the banners are changed according to the seasons, a long pole with a hook and a steady arm are essential.
- What is the banner trying to say? Images should be easily understood and not need words of explanation. A banner should inform, not puzzle.
- Is the banner going to be used in a procession? If so, it will need to be sturdily constructed.

Children of most ages can make simple banners. The easiest 'one off' is made with a drawing on A3 paper mounted on garden canes. Larger and less flimsy versions can be made in the same way, using A2-sized card with a collage to give more depth and texture than paint or felt-tipped pens. Children love making and using them in processions. Pictures of people and scenes from the gospels may be freely copied from *Short Cuts*,[4] OHP slides or any kind of artwork.

The same considerations of size and clarity must be applied to posters, friezes and any visual aids that may be used in church. Often a good idea is wasted because the picture is too small. This must be borne in mind when preparing material for an OHP or flip chart. The simplest images will be the ones that are most clearly remembered.

Visual aids for use in worship can also be made by people of all ages and abilities. Rather than a couple of adults preparing them beforehand, they can be made by children and adults working together as part of a Fun Day or meeting. The act of making them can, in itself, be part of the learning and worship process.

Chapter Eight

Movement and dance

Symbolic action

Symbols of all kinds appear in churches, in stained-glass windows, on banners, or carved in wood and stone. They remind us of the nature of God and the life of his Church. Symbolic actions can also be used in the Eucharist to show meanings which cannot be articulated so clearly in words. There is every reason to use movements in all-age worship when people at every stage of knowledge are present. Even a very young child can grasp the significance of a bowed head. A complete stranger might observe a dignified Gospel procession with candles and wonder why this particular book was so important. Actions like this can teach far more than the most eloquent preaching.

Both posture and gesture are important because people must be able to see as well as hear if their attention is to be held. Processions, actions during songs, and other activities all help to remind us that when we worship we offer our whole selves to God. Over-arching these is the modern understanding of liturgy in which we participate, stand, look and respond rather than spectate, kneel, bury our heads in a book or pew and keep silent. We learn best through using all of our senses. The postures we use in worship can teach us about our relationship with God and with each other. Making the sign of the cross, genuflecting or bowing at particular moments are gestures which portray emotion without words in any language being used.

Movement in the liturgy

Within the Eucharist there are many movements which communicate a deep meaning. The congregation standing together to sing at the beginning of a service demonstrates the unity of the people of God. This can be further emphasized if there is a big procession with banners on a feast day. A gospel procession with candles or the Bible being held high as it is taken to the pulpit or the centre of the church reminds us that Jesus comes among us in his Word and so we stand to honour him.

The Offertory is another time of movement as representatives of the people take bread and wine forward from the body of the church to represent the offering of the people's lives. Children may offer work done during their own Liturgy of the Word as part of this. At Harvest time or on Christmas morning this can be extended by the whole congregation moving forward to present gifts. Intercession for the sick could be accompanied by the laying on of hands or anointing in certain circumstances.

Standing, sitting and kneeling are also important, sitting being the most receptive, a time for listening and reflecting, and kneeling a time for humility and reverence. A bowed or uplifted head shows vividly the contrast between penitence and praise. A warm hand-shake at the Peace is one of the simplest but most effective movements used in the Eucharist. Strangers feel that they are part of the community after a hand clasp and a smile, even if they are on holiday and the whole service has been conducted in a foreign language.

The priest's gestures are of equal importance. The sign of the cross at the Greeting and Blessing, hands extended when saying, 'The Lord be with you', gestures made during the Eucharistic Prayer which strengthen the link between it and the Last Supper all speak clearly of the nature of God and his saving work among us.

Dance in worship

Dance has been used since the earliest times to celebrate the seasons and key events in people's lives such as weddings and funerals. Most of these dances were designed for participation by the whole community, whatever their age and status, rather than for performance to an audience.

That being the case, dance should find a natural home in all-age worship, yet why does the word, 'dance' not spring to the lips as quickly as 'music' or 'drama' when planning a liturgy? A possible answer lies in the Church's own history. Even though worshipping God through dancing is mentioned several times in the Old Testament, 'Praise him in the cymbals and dances' (Psalm 150) being a famous example, there is no record of dance being used in early Christian worship. The Church was aware that the emotional power of music could be a distraction rather than an aid to worship, and was even more wary of the sensual power of dance. Dance was linked with pagan ceremonies and a way of life that Christians renounced at baptism.

This tradition stayed with the Church. Music in dance form was not allowed to be performed in the church for centuries and all dancing anywhere was banned during the Commonwealth in seventeenth-century England. It is only recently with a rethinking of liturgical styles and a use of both folk and improvized dance in education that dancing has started to be used in Christian worship in this country.

Preparation

In most parishes the congregation will need to be gently introduced to the idea. However, if it is first explained that movement and gesture already play an important part in worship, dance can be seen as just one step further on. We worship God with our whole selves, and this includes bodily movement either on its own or as a response to music.

It is easiest to prepare a dance with a small group of mixed ages. Apart from it being difficult to organize a large group without disrupting the service, very few churches have enough space for a large group to move or be seen easily.

Timing is of the essence in dance. If the group is dancing to taped music, there is no problem, but if musicians are being used to accompany the dance it is vital that they play for as many of the rehearsals as possible. The best compromise is for the musicians to attend one of the first rehearsals and then make a tape recording to be used at other sessions to assure consistency of tempo. A final run-through can then sort out any small modifications and check that the speed is still correct. A fraction of a second's difference is not noticeable to the casual listener but can make a dance look heavy and clumsy – or, more probably, leave the dancers breathless as the tendency is usually for musicians to play too fast.

Creating dances

The thought of creating a dance for use in worship fills most people with even more horror than providing music. They recognize the skill needed and feel that, without a high level of expertise, they cannot do anything. However, there may be more skill lurking in the pews than is expected. Anyone who has taken part in light opera or musicals will know the kind of simple routines that are used with great effect and can move on from that basis. Creative dance is often taught in school so, as with young musicians, there may well be skilled dancers and choreographers within the congregation.

Getting ideas is always the hardest part. Look at some hymns and songs to see if they lend themselves to movement. Quite often a simple pattern of movements arises from the words of a refrain as in this popular harvest hymn:

> *All good gifts around us* (Stretch out the right arm to the front and turn around in a circle.)
> *Are sent from heaven above.* (Put arms up straight, palms turned upwards and look up.)
> *Then thank the Lord,* (Bring straightened arms down in front, still with palms upwards.)
> *O thank the Lord* (Beckon hands towards you.)
> *For all his love.* (Extend hands to the sides.)

The melody of a hymn or song can also spark an idea for a dance. Then it is best to work out the pattern and try it on your own with an accompaniment before introducing it to your group. This way, any problems can be ironed out before the rehearsal. Nothing is more irritating or confusing than waiting while the director recreates his or her ideas.

Congregational movement and dance

The above suggestions are concerned with using a group of dancers, but many early ritual dances involved the whole community. The suggestion than a whole congregation could dance during a liturgy conjures up visions of chaos: 'We can't have dancing in church – nobody does; how would you know when to stop? how would you get back to your seat?' Of course, many charismatic churches do use dance in this way and find it a fulfilling way of worshipping. A starting point might be to suggest that the congregation might sing or pray with hands uplifted. Youngsters will join in with gusto, some adults will find it liberating to lose the traditional hands clasped position of praying and the more inhibited will gradually be encouraged to join in.

If movement is going to be used, it must be clear and positive. A whole congregation holding its arms up to sing 'Alleluia' on Easter morning can look and feel very exciting. A limp hand and bent arm barely raised to shoulder height looks what it is – half-hearted. If you are going to express God's sovereignty over the whole world by making the shape of a circle, let it be a big one, arms up over the head and then stretched out, if space permits. This boldness is even more important if gestures are taught in a short practice before the service. An apologetic demonstration will result in half-hearted movements and most of the congregation opting out when the time comes.

The most common time for using a corporate dance pattern is during the Lord's Prayer. Jane Miller, from our family in the Introduction, was moved when she saw the children lift up their hands as they sang it. In another church they may have gone a little further and prayed with gestures such as these:

Our Father (Hold hands forward with palms upwards.)
Who art in Heaven, (Lift hands slowly to chin height.)
Hallowed be thy name. (Bow head, leaving hands still.)
Thy kingdom come, (Look upwards.)
Thy will be done (Put arms straight above head.)
On earth (Bring arms round in a circle and down to sides.)
As it is in heaven. (Hold hands forward with palms upwards.)

Give us this day our daily bread, (Make a bowl with cupped hands.)
And forgive us our trespasses (Fold hands on chest and bow head.)
As we forgive those who trespass against us. (Hold hands out to
   the sides and turn head to each side in turn.)
Lead us not into temptation, (Arms in front with palms forward as
   if pushing something away, and head turned half away.)
But deliver us from evil. (Arms crossed over chest.)

For the kingdom, (Put arms straight above head and look up.)
The power and the glory are yours (Brings arms round in a circle
   and down to the sides.)
Now and for ever. (Hands forward as at the beginning of the prayer.)

Whatever you plan, the motto is to keep it simple. The suggested movements to accompany the Lord's Prayer have four basic patterns which are repeated as appropriate:

- Hands are held forward in a petitioning position at the beginning, the end, and when asking for daily bread.
- God's kingship is illustrated by a circle.
- A bowed head depicts reverence and penitence.
- Strength and adoration are shown by arms being put straight above the head.
  Similar movements are used in the dance for the harvest hymn.

Any movement or dance should be intended to enhance the worship, to emphasize a scriptural or liturgical point or to lead to prayer. A badly performed dance or feeble movements will do none of these but will merely draw attention to the performers' weaknesses whereas a simple pattern done well can be truly uplifting.

Within the Eucharist

There are two particular places where dance can be used during the Eucharist, at the Offertory and after Communion. If it is used at the Offertory, some of the many folk dances which are connected with work, harvest or the offering of gifts might provide a starting point from which to build a specifically Christian dance. The English Folk Dance and Song Society[1] have booklets on their work in this region while *Steps of Faith*[2] is a practical introduction to using dance in worship. There are also numerous dances on these subjects from other cultures which children may learn at school and enjoy doing,[3] thus adding a rich new dimension to the worship.

The time immediately after receiving Holy Communion is one of quiet prayer and reflection. A calm, flowing dance could be used here with a quiet accompaniment to set the atmosphere. In contrast, after a period of stillness and quiet, the final hymn could be an ideal time to have a celebratory dance. This could be one of the best points to introduce dance in worship to the congregation as it can be seen as the summing up of a celebration when people are seen literally to dance with joy. It can be short and to the point. Maybe some of the congregation will even start to join in by moving and clapping their hands.

Chapter Nine

Outreach

Getting started

Many churches will have already pursued some of the suggestions made in this book. If your parish has not done so, do not attempt to deal with every area in one fell swoop. A gentle evolution is usually better than a sudden change of almost every feature of the liturgy and can be combined with teaching and explanation. For a congregation that has a very traditional pattern of worship, and is perhaps still resistant to the very idea of children being actively involved, it may be best to concentrate for a few months on having an introduction to the readings and short illustrated sermon. Children can be involved in the Offertory on a week when they have their own Liturgy of the Word. Posture for prayer can be reviewed at another time, and so on.

In a parish that has always welcomed children and visitors to the Eucharist and is used to their taking part as musicians, readers and intercessors, it will be better to review the whole liturgy, stage by stage, and see where there are sections that need developing or restructuring.

Whatever plans are made, it is vital to look at every aspect of worship, not just at what is spoken or sung. Changes of posture always take up time and cause a certain disruption, so having several sections of worship in one position rather than constant changes from standing to sitting or kneeling gives the liturgy a better flow. It is also easier for the majority of worshippers, especially for those who are infirm or are looking after young children. Kneeling for all the prayers is quite a strain for many people, and, on a strictly practical note, most churches had their pews installed during the last century when people were shorter, so kneeling is very cramping for tall people in the majority of churches. If it is reserved for the Eucharistic Prayer, it has the added advantage of highlighting the solemnity of this part of the liturgy.

The use of books and booklets need careful consideration. They can cause distraction and confusion. Modern copying techniques make it easy to compile an attractive booklet which contains all the information necessary, including instructions on standing, sitting and kneeling for use in the service. Nothing is more embarrassing than for visitors in the front row to glance round to find the whole congregation has knelt while they are still standing. Brief information on receiving Holy Communion or a blessing can also be given. All this can be illustrated with simple graphics.

Some parishes use commercially printed booklets of the text of the Eucharist and provide a notice leaflet which has the special prayers and readings to go with it. For special occasions, this could be combined with a full service booklet, even with the hymns included, so that just one item could be given out, followed and taken home afterwards. Once the basic format has been set up, it is simple to add the date, hymns and even extra information, for example, 'Readings and prayers led by the St Mary's Scouts', or 'Family Eucharist with the Baptism of Anthony David Jenkins'. Equally, we have to look critically at our use of timing and silence. There is a world of difference between the planned silence for prayer and reflection after a reading and the silence which is just an absence of sound while the reader walks to the lectern and finds his or her place in the Bible. The latter sets up tension rather than encouraging a receptive mood and centres attention upon the reader rather than the reading.

All people respond to atmosphere and our liturgy must be worthy of the mystery it proclaims and be seen to be significant and authentic. Many conservatively minded members of the congregation and not a few clergy fear that all-age worship will be superficial and banal. Experience suggests that it can often lead to a greater sense of God's presence and of worshipping as a community among both adults and children. It is also a successful vehicle for both teaching the faith and alerting people to the Church's role in the world.

Evangelization and the Eucharist

'We are gathered together as God's family ...' These or similar words introduce the Eucharist Sunday by Sunday in churches all over the country. But is this the time when the whole family gathers or is it still a celebration for the eclectic few? Is it possible for fringe members of the Church to be made to feel genuinely part of this celebration?

It has been argued that the Eucharist is exclusive by its very nature and historical background, that those who are not in the centre of the family feel unchurched, and even that it is not part of our outreach to the secular world. In the early Church as in other contemporary cults, exclusiveness was an attraction and, under persecution, a necessity for survival. In Britain today, however, our problem is not persecution but being seen as irrelevant to today's world, as dull and ineffective.

We have shown in the preceding chapters of this book that Eucharistic worship need not be obscure and can convey a sense of mystery and celebration that will challenge any suggestion of dullness or exclusivity. The view is increasingly held that worship is the 'shop window' of the Christian Church. In this Decade of Evangelization, mission must start rather than end with worship for it is in worshipping God that we come to know our true selves. We put ourselves in the presence of God through prayer, signs and symbols, studying the Scriptures and serving others. Although aspects of worship can be practised anywhere and at any time, they are all combined to the fullest degree in the Eucharist. The effective all-age Parish Eucharist will present these challenges and opportunities in a way that can be grasped by each worshipper, from the mystic to the person on the edge of belief.

A priest who had a weekly Eucharist as part of his ministry to down-and-outs once commented on the importance of sharing the Peace: '... for it was the only time that these people were touched'. An elderly widow, living alone, described having her name used by the priest as he gave her Holy Communion, 'like a light caress'. This also applies to young people. The corporate sharing of the Peace is not just a social greeting but has a sacramental dimension in that it is an expression of our unity as the Body of Christ and members of one another. The handclasp and smile may bring more comfort to a lonely or troubled youngster than the fellowship of 'coffee in the hall afterwards'.

Teenage Confirmation is an evangelistic opportunity that is often wasted since many youngsters in their early teens attend classes with enthusiasm, only to disappear a year later. These same youngsters are discovering their own identity as well as being under a lot of pressure to pass exams, get a job or decide on a course of training for the future. Pop stars, friendships and fashions change overnight, so it is hardly surprising that religion, if it is not well-grounded and celebrated as part of a living community, is thrown out when other crazes and pressures turn up. But this can be a time of spiritual growth as well. While a youngster is asking, 'Who am I?' he may also be asking, 'Who is God?' While he has his heroes and villains, he can also be seeing how Jesus, great saints, and, indeed, his local Church leaders match up in comparison. Interest in politics and current affairs may also lead to a scrutiny of the Church's role in an unjust or impoverished society. Clergy and religious publishers are beginning to become aware of the need for a properly structured course for young people and several excellent complete courses, *Meet Christ with Joy*,[1] *Lifeline*[2] and *Calling You*[3] have been published during the last few years, as well as books for older teenagers such as *Confirmation to Follow*.[4]

Having centred our evangelization literally on the altar, it then radiates out into the world and draws people together to share in our family meal. There will be a place at the Eucharist for not only the youngest in years, but also for the new Christian, the enquirer, and those who are on the edge of the Church either for lack of commitment or because they are also on the fringe of society.

Involving the fringe

The very structure of an all-age Eucharist with its opportunities for drama, varied visual aids and music, can draw in people who are on the fringe of the church by incorporating their talents, professions or membership of a particular club. On a simple level, a uniformed organization like the Guides, which will have non-church people among its members, can be asked to provide readers, lead the intercessions or take part in the Offertory procession. One of the clergy or lay leaders may plan the intercessions with the group at a meeting, thus getting an opportunity to know the youngsters and their leaders, discuss issues that are in the media, items for concern or thanksgiving and personal needs such as family illness or worry about exams, as well as explaining the content and theme of the readings. Taken further, a group could provide a drama, musical accompaniment, decoration or visual aids according to the talents available, thus drawing in people who have a particular skill or interest. This has been described in detail in the chapters on music, drama, visual aids and dance.

Groups need not only be recognizable organizations such as the Youth Club or the Mothers' Union. People who live in a particular street or, in certain circumstances, the family and friends of a baptismal candidate can contribute in the same way and draw in a variety of ages and talents as well as involving people who rarely come to church. However, it is always important to think through the selection of any particular group. For example, it might seem ideal to use a single family – three generations of Jones's preparing the intercessions together is a wonderful image. In practice, it might be highly insensitive and pastorally disastrous in that it creates a certain complacency within the 'perfect family' while forcing a sense of loss on those whose families are incomplete through death or divorce or where lack of faith or pressure of shift-work prevent a family worshipping together. Particular talents and skills can be used in different ways of leading prayers, asking for petitions to be sent in advance to a particular leader or using a flip chart to collect suggestions are two of many. Other examples can be found in *All Age Worship*[5] an invaluable hand book dealing with all aspects of the subject.

Eucharistic worship away from the church building

So far, we have discussed the all-age Eucharist almost entirely, in the context of the main Sunday worship. However, there are many other situations in which the principles of such worship may be used with great benefit to all concerned. Within small groups such as the Youth Club or a house group there is scope for liturgical experiment as well as introducing people to the worship in a more relaxed setting. New readers and intercessors will find it less daunting to speak in a large gothic building with a couple of hundred people present if they have already gained experience in front of a dozen friends in a small chapel or room.

With greater ease of travel and car ownership, parish weekends with a varied programme for each age group are becoming increasingly popular. Here, as in Youth Club holidays or Scout camps, there is an ideal opportunity for part of the Church family to celebrate the Eucharist with a new awareness of the value of friendships formed and relationships strengthened during the time spent together. It is often a moving experience for even the most experienced church members to receive Holy Communion in the context of their holiday – for a boat cabin, a tent or a field to be seen to be a holy place. If a priest is not available, a simple 'agape' service with sharing of bread and wine can still remind all partakers of their unity with Christ and the many meals he shared with his disciples.

Eucharists for children

A children's Eucharist is slightly different because here children will be in the majority and the number of adults present may be very small. An example of this would be a concluding Eucharist at a children's Fun Day in a parish, deanery or diocese, or at any special occasion that has brought groups of children together. When children form the Eucharistic community in this way, the approach to their participation will be quite different from that in a parish situation. They can be invited to do much more, to take responsibility for the preparation and serving, reading, interceding, and clearing away – tasks which would be shared if all ages were present.

To some degree, the teaching elements can be focused on a particular age group though, as Chapter Two implied, a group that spans a relatively small age range will contain enormous differences in perception and understanding. If there is a regular children's Eucharist, for example at a Saturday club, the planning will need to relate both to Sunday worship and also to the teaching content of any programme in use at regular meetings.

School Eucharists

A Eucharist in school will probably include many children who are not worshipping members of their own church communities, some from other faiths and a number who resist the idea of religious affinities or belief altogether. The age range may well be narrow at a school Eucharist but the range of background experience will generally be very wide. There is enormous evangelistic potential in this kind of celebration if it is handled sensitively.

In planning school Eucharists, there may be a relationship with what is going on in the local parish though most children are unlikely to attend the parish church; there may also be a relationship with teaching programmes and themes so that classes can contribute to the liturgy in various ways. It is important, however, that the school Eucharist does not become overburdened by formal teaching, nor that it seems to be used only to reinforce classroom RE. Books like *Keep it in the Family*[6] and *Family Mass Themes*[7] give topics which can act as a good basis for any school celebration.

When planning music, drama and other aspects of presentation there is likely to be a wide variety of talent to be drawn on from both staff and pupils. Perhaps one of the most truly all-age Eucharists was not held in a church but in a school hall upon the headteacher's retirement. The congregation of some five hundred ranged from a bishop to the youngest brothers and sisters of pupils. Committed Christians sat side by side with families of other religions and no religion at all. Pupils and staff were involved throughout with the hymns accompanied by the school orchestra and led by the pupils' and parents' joint choir with a dance for the Offertory and voluntaries by a jazz band.

This kind of presentation requires much hard work and forethought. A simple Eucharist needs less rehearsal and amount of work, but a similar attitude will be richly rewarded. A haphazard approach and low standards of expectation will result in lost opportunities and create depression. Planning and co-operation are essential if the school

Eucharist is truly to gather together people and concerns, and to express before God the life of the community.

The family service

Having emphasized the inclusiveness of the Eucharist and practical ways in which it can be planned, the question that follows must be, 'Is there no place for other Family worship?' The answer is, 'Of course there is!' There is a need for short acts of worship such as pram services for hard-pressed mothers with babies and toddlers, a crib service on Christmas Eve or a simple Way of the Cross on Good Friday. Informal services modelled on worship at Taizé or Iona, local, maybe ecumenical *Songs of Praise*, Christingles, carol festivals and processions have an everlasting appeal to a wide range of people both in the centre and on the fringe of Church life. Each and every parish should encourage and promote any form of worshipping God and celebrating his love for us.

Chapter Ten

Ideas and illustrations

Each of the following presentations was planned with a particular Sunday or festival in mind and is based on either the Bible readings or the topic in the title. They range from being continuous commentaries on the day's readings or simple talks with a few visual aids to ways in which children can use their work within the liturgy. Most of them have suggested Bible readings which fit with the topic as it was originally planned. Where alternatives or other uses are given, this can be done with little or no adaptation.

1. An All Saints-tide presentation of the Christian life
2. The Body of Christ
3. The bread and the wine
4. The good news of the covenant
5. The Good Shepherd
6. Love God and love your neighbour
7. A light to lighten the Gentiles
8. The light that would not be blown out
9. A present for Jesus
10. The sin tree
11. A Saint Francis' Harvest presentation
12. Sending out the apostles
13. Simultaneous translation
14. The Way of the Cross with movement and actions
15. What is coming? Who is coming?

1. An All Saints-tide presentation of the Christian life

This is complete in itself as a simple non-eucharistic liturgy to be used at the end of a children's Fun Day. It could also be adapted for use at an all-age Eucharist if the preparation section were done during a previous Sunday's Ministry of the Word or at a weekday club.

Uses

- All Saints-tide (1 November)
- Patronal festival
- Anniversary of dedication
- Baptism preparation or follow-up

Bible readings

Matthew 5:1–12
1 John 3:1–3
Revelation 7:2–4, 9–14

Preparation

Ask or take the children to look around the church at saints' representations in windows and statues. Teach them about their own name or birthday saint and maybe draw the symbol associated with him or her. The traditional signs for most saints are shown in *Saints, Signs and Symbols*.[1] Decorate jam jars with cut-out paper wrapped around the jar with symbols of their saints and of the Christian faith. Put a night-light inside each one. This idea is adapted from one in *We always put a Candle in the Window*.[2]

Presentation

The action falls into three sections which could be a continuous liturgy in itself with readings included, or take the place of the homily involving the congregation turning towards or moving around parts of the church building.

1. Start at the font and ask everyone to imagine themselves as tiny babies, as being born and being baptized. Each of us is formed according to the living purpose of God and a new life begins at baptism. Renew the baptismal vows (asking the unbaptized people present to look forward to the time when they will make them),

and light the lamps from the Paschal Candle which is seated beside the font, its recommended place outside the Easter season.

2. Process as God's People singing a song to the chapel where the Blessed Sacrament is reserved. If the Blessed Sacrament is not reserved in your church, process to a point where an open Bible is displayed. After discussion of the many helps God gives his people on their journey, pause for prayer, remembering especially the lapsed and the lost.

3. Continue the procession to the main altar and place the lamps on and around it as signs of our sharing, at the end of our earthly life, in the heavenly banquet with Jesus in the midst. This could then be concluded with prayers of thanksgiving, or, if this takes place within the Eucharist, it would be the most natural thing to keep the children around the altar with their lamps, near to the signs of the eucharistic presence of Jesus in bread and wine.

2.　The Body of Christ

The theme of this talk is, 'We are all of one body'. It aims to show that the Church is made up of people with different talents and tasks, but that, moreover, all our talents are of equal importance in the service of the Christ and the world.

Uses

● ASB Lectionary:　Pentecost 7, Year 1
　　　　　　　　　　Pentecost 8, Year 2
　　　　　　　　　　Pentecost 18, Year 2
● Three-Year Lectionary:　33rd Sunday, Year A
　　　　　　　　　　　　　2nd Sunday, Year C

Bible readings

Any of St Paul's writings about our being the Body of Christ:
Romans 12:4–8
1 Corinthians 12:12–31
Ephesians 4:11–16

Parable of the Talents:
Matthew 25:14–30

Equipment

● Two A2 sheets of cardboard
● Thick felt-tipped pens (for clarity of reading)
● A display board or a large piece of paper that can be hung up after the homily
● Sticky tack or drawing pins

Preparation

Cut out from the card a large outline of a person. Unless you are very artistic, the easiest way to do this is by drawing round a child who is lying on the card. Write across it in large letters, 'WE ARE THE BODY OF CHRIST', then cut the outline up into pieces to make a simple 'jigsaw puzzle'. Before the service, arrange to have a display board near to the chancel step or a large piece of paper lying ready to be hung on a nearby wall or from a pillar.

Presentation

Start by complimenting the congregation on their singing. (This could be replaced by any talent that is evident in the church that morning such as a flower arrangement, or by thanking people who had, for example, organized a social event or weeded the churchyard recently. The aim is to be aware of the talents that are present in the church.) Ask who enjoys singing or whatever talent has been mentioned and then invite one of the people who responded to come out, write his or her name and the talent on a piece of jigsaw and hold it up. Gradually collect various names and talents, not forgetting the vital ones of being cheerful and willing to help with chores like tidying bedrooms. When the pieces have all been distributed, ask the volunteers to put them together on the board and discover that they make the figure of a body, with, 'WE ARE THE BODY OF CHRIST' written across it. Point out that the Body is, in fact, John who helped look after his little brother, Anne who is a bell-ringer etc., and that, just as a body with five legs and no head would be incomplete, so would the Body of Christ be unable to function properly if we valued some people and their talents while discounting others.

This talk could be given at the traditional time but it could also be used as an introduction to the Epistle or be placed after the Creed and lead straight into Intercessions on the same topic. A children's story, *Frederick* by Leo Leoni[3] would also make an excellent commentary on this for younger children.

At the sign of Peace the whole congregation could repeat together, 'We are the Body of Christ' before sharing the Peace.

3.   The bread and the wine

This is a presentation before the Offertory which aims to help members of the congregation to see it as a moment to offer their whole selves and lives to God as the president is preparing the bread and wine. It would be possible to extend this to a continuous presentation running through the Ministry of the Word.

Uses

- Harvest
- Teaching on the Eucharist
- Any occasion celebrating our membership of the Body of Christ.

Bible readings

No special readings

Equipment

- Costumes for the various characters
- A large chalice
- A loaf or large altar breads laid visibly on a paten or ciborium

Preparation

A simple outline script needs to be written and a brief rehearsal with the people concerned is required.

The first part of the script presents the story of bread from the sowing of the seed to the baking. The farmer sows the seed, his workers fertilize the ground, the driver combine-harvests it, the workers bag it, the lorry driver takes it to the mill, the miller grinds it, the baker (or monk/nun) bakes it, the van driver delivers it to the church. The bread of the Eucharist is thus identified with human labour as well as being food.

The second half presents various human celebrations at which wine is drunk in celebration – 'Wine that makes glad the heart of man' – a wedding reception (a bridal couple), a sports club (tennis whites), an 18th birthday disco (pop clothes), a business man (dark suits) etc. Wine is identified with rejoicing.

Presentation

As the script is read, each character dressed in the appropriate costume comes up and stands round the altar, beginning on the president's right and spreading outwards for the work; for the celebrations beginning on the president's left in the same way. At the end of reading the script, there will be a semi-circle of figures round the altar. The bread and wine may then be brought up from the congregation with quiet musical accompaniment and it is especially appropriate for the president to say the Offertory Prayers:

Blessed are you Lord God of all creation, through your goodness we have this bread to offer which earth has given and human hands have made, it will become for us the bread of life.

Blessed are you Lord God of all creation, through your goodness we have this wine to offer, fruit of the vine and work of human hands, it will become our spiritual drink.

to which all respond:

Blessed be God for ever.

Alternatively the song, 'Blessed are you Lord God of all creation' (*Celebration Hymnal* 410)[4] may be sung at this point with an additional verse:

Blessed are you Lord God of all creation,
Thanks to your goodness ourselves we offer
People of yours, made by your hands,
Take us and use us as your own.

The characters can remain round the altar during the Eucharistic Prayer if this is thought appropriate.

4. The good news of the covenant

This project involves advance preparation by several people from within the parish. The aim is to remind us of the pact of love that God made with each of us at our baptism.

Uses

- Promises
- Baptism
- Conversion
- ASB Lectionary: Sunday after Epiphany, Years 1 and 2
                  Pentecost 3, Year 1
- Three-Year Lectionary: First Sunday of Lent, Year B

Bible readings

Genesis 9:8–15 (the rainbow)
1 Peter 3:18–22 (baptismal reflection on the flood)
Mark 1:12–15 (John the Baptist proclaiming repentance).

The aim is to teach the progression of Christian Initiation.

Preparation

Decorate the church with heads of animals, an elephant's trunk, lion's head, etc., peeping from behind the pillars, from the pulpit and behind the lectern. The aim is to help the congregation to feel they are in Noah's Ark.

Make a long strip of crepe paper in the colours of the rainbow. If possible, arrange for a pulley so that it can be raised at the east end of the church and hung across the sanctuary. If this is impossible, get a group of people to hold it up at the right times and then fix it to the east wall. These are the sort of craft activities that the Youth Club or a group of Young Mothers may be able to do.

Have three large cards with, COVENANT, BAPTISM and REPENT written on them. Have a jug of water ready beside the font.

Presentation

Introduce the Old Testament reading by singing the chorus, 'Who built the Ark?' (*Someone's Singing, Lord*) or a similar song about Noah[5] and by the reader reminding the congregation that, after the flood,

God sent a sign of his friendship with his creatures. At the words, 'God said, "Here is the sign of the covenant ..."' raise the crepe-paper rainbow up from the floor at the east end of the church and hang it across the sanctuary. At the end of the reading, ask a child to hold up the COVENANT card.

Before the New Testament reading, go to the font and give a brief explanation of the symbolism of baptism as washing clean, linking this to the flood, before pouring a jug of water from a height into the font. Follow this with the reading and, at the end, get someone to hold up the key word, BAPTISM.

Before the Gospel, ask for volunteers to line up at the chancel step with their backs to the congregation. Explain how, in the early Church, the candidates at baptism faced the west wall of the church and literally turned round to show their 'turning to Christ'. As the line of people demonstrate this, hold up the key word, REPENT.

After the Gospel, just take a couple of minutes to point out the progression into the Christian life, using the key words in reverse order: 'REPENT, be BAPTISED, and live the COVENANT'. Get everyone to repeat them. It might be a good idea to repeat them again before the Blessing at the end of the service.

5. The Good Shepherd

This is an illustrated talk but it can be extended into a continuous commentary if the theme of sheep and the Good Shepherd is expanded.

Uses

- Sundays in Eastertide, especially 'Good Shepherd Sunday'
- ASB lectionary: Easter 4, Years A B and C

Bible readings

Ezekiel 34:7–16
Psalm 23
John 10:1–10, 7–16, 11–18, 27–30
1 Peter 2:20–25
Revelation 7:14–17

Equipment

A shepherd's crook. This can be bought from some hikers' and outdoor shops or made from a length of dowelling with a cardboard or wire hook nailed to the top.

Preparatiom

Nil

Presentation

A shepherd uses his crook to move sheep by nudging them with it or putting the hook round a hind leg. Move round the congregation, using the shepherd's crook against or round people's arms to draw out those who have particular ministries in the Church. Take care to cover a representative group: musicians, readers, servers, those who care for the church building, carers, cleaners, etc. See that you include one or two with 'hidden' skills of prayer, and one or two who simply come to church. Develop the idea, 'I know my sheep' – Jesus knows what we can do. The risen Christ lives in his church and cares for his flock. He brings us back when we stray. He knows us by name and wants to encourage us to do his will for the building up of the whole Church.

In cases of the infirm or very young, it might be wiser to ask them to grasp the crook, an act which in itself would be a powerful symbol of acceptance.

Depending on the other readings used on the day, the theme of the Church as the Lord's flock could be developed. Prayer for the clergy and lay ministers as shepherds of the flock could follow the reading from Ezekiel. If Psalm 23 or Revelation 7 are used, then the idea that Jesus calls us out for eternal life might be developed.

6. Love God and love your neighbour

This theme can be expanded in several places during the Eucharist or put together as a single talk. It shows how we receive God's love and reflect it in our love for each other.

Uses

As a commentary on any readings which include the Ten Commandments or Summary of the Law; also on the Gospel readings from the Sermon on the Mount or any readings on God's great love for us.

Bible readings

Deuteronomy 6:1–11
Mark 12:28–34
Matthew 5:38–48
Luke 6:27–38

Equipment

- A large torch
- A disc of cardboard as big as the torch's glass
- Several small mirrors
- Pictures or slides of an eclipse of the sun (optional)

Preparation

Have the equipment close at hand. Arrange for someone to turn the lights on and off. If you decide to use pictures or slides, have them displayed or ready for showing.

Presentation

After the opening hymn and greeting, explain that the sun is the original source of light in our world. The moon and planets have no light of their own but reflect the sun's light. An eclipse of the sun is caused when the moon passes between the sun and earth and so prevents the sun's light reaching us. Use a strong torch beam to represent the sun and pass a disc of cardboard slowly across it to show how the moon blocks out the light, or get people to walk slowly in front of the beam for similar effect.

Explain how God's love is like the sun. We can receive it and reflect it or we can let sin, like the moon, come between us and God's love. Introduce the penitential rite by inviting the congregation to call to mind the things that come between us and God and the times that we have let sin be a block or have turned away from the light of his love. You could use the baptismal question, 'Do you turn to Christ? I turn to Christ' with the congregation turning from the back of the church towards the altar at this point as shown in sample 4, The Good News of the Covenant.

After the Gospel, invite several people to come forward holding small mirrors. Using the torch beam as God's love again, get them to use the mirrors to reflect the light around the church and on to particular people. Ask how we can reflect God's love for us in the ways that we behave towards each other. Conclude by saying together, 'Shine as a light in the world to the glory of God the Father'.

When the Peace is introduced, you could get the mirror beams trained around the congregation again before it shares the Peace and then turn on the brightest lights in the church for the rest of the service while singing, 'This little light of mine' or 'Lord the light of your love is shining' (*Celebration Hymnal* nos 329 and 768).

7. A light to lighten the Gentiles

More parishes have started having a Sung Eucharist to celebrate the Presentation of the Lord (or Candlemas) in recent years. *The Promise of his Glory* includes suggestions for a Service of Light and a Eucharist of Candlemas, though it would be more in keeping with the Gospel story to have the procession at the beginning of the service, rather that at the end as suggested in it.

Whatever time you choose, children will enjoy taking part in a candle-lit procession which acts out the Lord coming to the temple. The Gospel is a vivid one and the flickering light has a drama of its own so it is not necessary to arrange any complicated homily. Let the candles and the Gospel reading speak for themselves. There are, however, a couple of ways in which the children can prepare for this feast beforehand and share their work with the rest of the congregation in the liturgy.

Uses

● Presentation of the Lord (2 February)
● Jesus, the light of the Word
● Saints, as reflections of Jesus's light

Bible readings

Luke 2:22–35
Matthew 5:14–16
Malachi 3:1–4
Psalm 24

Equipment

Candle lanterns
● Jam jars
● Night lights or very short candles
● Plasticine or 'blu-tak'
● Scissors
● String

Preparation

Attach a *long* string handle to the top of each jam jar. This is for safety and to prevent people getting burned. Stick a night light or candle into each jar with plasticine or melted wax and *lay it sideways* to light it.

Candle cards
● Pieces of yellow or gold paper, about A5 size
● Coloured shapes of sticky paper (optional)
● Felt-tipped pens

Preparation

Make a candle card by drawing a curved line and a candle flame at the top of the short side of a piece of yellow or gold paper. Cut it out and fold the piece of paper length ways so that the flame is on the inside. Colour the flame red or orange and decorate the front with sticky shapes or felt-tipped pens. Write inside, 'Jesus is the Light of the World'. It is quickest to make a cardboard template beforehand and let the children draw round it.

Presentation

Arrange for some of the children to assist the sidesmen before the service and give a card to each person as they arrive.

Carry the lanterns into church at the beginning of the service and place them around the altar at the Offertory.

Music

As in no. 6, 'This little light of mine' or 'Shine, Jesus, shine' (*Celebration Hymnal*) are suitable songs for this service.

8.   The light that would not be blown out

This short activity for Easter Day uses the simple but vivid image of an everlasting candle to illustrate Jesus's death and resurrection.

Uses

Any Sunday during the Easter season

Equipment

● A packet of everlasting candles
● Several small potatoes
● A tray of sand
● Matches

Preparation

Make the potatoes into candle holders by cutting them in half and making a hole in the curved part and pressing a candle into each one. Place them on a small table near the chancel steps with a tray of sand nearby. This preparation is a safety measure as everlasting candles are very difficult to extinguish. The damp potato will form a safe candle holder if the candle burns right down and the sand is there for emergency. Arrange to have someone to give out the lighted candles and a sidesman to put out the church lights at the right moment.

Presentation

Start by asking the congregation what happened on the first Easter Day. Then ask them what sort of person Jesus was – teacher, healer, loving etc. For each answer, get someone to come out and hold one of the lighted candles. When they are all lit, ask for the church lights to be turned off so that the candles are seen to be shining brightly. Explain briefly how Jesus was like this light shining in a dark world. Say, 'Then on Good Friday, Jesus was crucified and the light was blown out'. Invite the people to blow out their candles and stand still. Within a few seconds, the candles should relight, illustrating that nothing can extinguish Jesus' life and light.

9.   A present for Jesus

After the hectic round of Christmas celebrations, Epiphany can get missed out because it is there before we have recovered! It is such a rich festival, full of symbolism, that it is a pity if we only celebrate it by singing a few special hymns. There are two simple themes that can be taken from the Gospel for Epiphany: the gifts and the star. Of these, the gifts can be featured in a short homily which is linked with the Offertory. The first part of it can be used as a teaching session or even in a school assembly.

Uses

Epiphany or the following Sunday

Bible reading

Matthew 2:1–12

Equipment

- Something made of gold, preferably a gold plated chalice. A ring can also be used, but is rather small.
- A thurible of incense
- A flagon of oil, preferably scented with balsam

NB Please try to use the real thing, not a paper crown and a joss stick. Friar's Balsam is available from most chemists.

Preparation

Nothing is essential apart from collecting the above but if you are really keen, dress three men or children as the three wise men.

Presentation

If your church does not use incense, have a smouldering thurible placed on a small table near to the back of the church. Smell is the most evocative of the senses and the incense will immediately set a different atmosphere and heighten a sense of expectancy.

Start the homily by having the three gifts displayed in clear view, not forgetting to ask someone to bring forward the incense. Let some of the children handle the gold, watch the smoke rise from the incense and smell the myrrh. Ask by whom or when these things are used and explain how the gifts are in themselves symbolic. The gold reminds us that Jesus is a King. Incense has been used while offering prayers to God for centuries in several religions so it reminds us that Jesus is God. People will probably find it hard to find a use for myrrh so you will have to explain that it is used in embalming bodies, showing that Jesus was destined to suffer and die for us.

If you want to develop this by showing how we use these elements in worship today, point out that we try to have our chalice and altar vessels made of precious metal and that incense is used in many churches. If your church uses incense, this is easy; if it does not, you might consider using it for just this feast as a reminder that we worship God with *all* of our senses – and that includes smell. Myrrh can be mentioned by explaining briefly a little about the use of oil in the rite of healing.

To round this off, let the 'Three Kings' or any three people present the gifts at the altar with the rest of the Offertory procession and use the hymn, 'Bethlehem of noblest cities' (translated as 'Earth has many a noble city' in some books) at some time during the rest of the service as one verse describes the meaning of the gifts.

10. The sin tree

This forms an extended Penitential section which can also be used on its own as part of an assembly or act of worship to illustrate teaching on sin and forgiveness. The activity helps the participants to recognize the many aspects of sin, including society's failings and the injustices of the world order. It teaches that, when we hear the words of God's forgiveness, something transforming happens and new life is made possible.

Uses

Any Sunday, but those in Lent and Eastertide are especially appropriate.

Bible readings

Any suitable readings on the theme

Equipment

- A large branch which can be made to stand up like a tree in itself, built into a suitable base or firmly bedded in a tub
- Brown paper
- Pencils
- Scissors
- Sticky tack or similar fixings which will only stick very lightly
- Coloured tissue paper
- Thread or fine string

Preparation

Make leaves out of brown paper big enough to write on. Make flowers out of tissue paper (which need not be particularly carefully made as they will make their impact from a distance). Attach pieces of thread to them so that they can be hung on to the tree easily when the time comes.

In groups beforehand (or this may be done during the liturgy if time permits) ask the young people and adults to think about sins that they can identify – personal but also social – and write one on each brown leaf.

Have a group of children rehearsed in 'operating' the tree.

Presentation

The leaves are fixed *very lightly* on the tree while some of the sins are read out. An appropriate prayer of confession, litany or other form is used by everyone to acknowledge and confess their sins. When the priest says the prayer for forgiveness, the tree is shaken violently by a group of children until all the brown leaves of sin have fallen off. Further explanation is given: forgiveness leads to new life, an experience of dying to sin leads to resurrection. The attractive coloured flowers are hung on the tree as a visual sign of new life after forgiveness. This can be done by the children, but if the congregation is not very large, everyone can come forward in a procession to put their flower on the tree while some simple music (like a Taizé chant) is played or sung.

11.   A Saint Francis' Harvest presentation

This is an alternative to using the usual Harvest images. Instead, try approaching Harvest Thanksgiving through an appreciation of the life and work of St Francis.

Uses

- Harvest Thanksgiving
- St Francis-tide (4 October)
- One World week (last week in October)

Bible readings

Genesis 1:1–15 (God creates the world, and it is good.)
Hebrews 2:9–11 (The one who sanctifies and those who are sanctified are from the same stock.)
Matthew 10:7–13 (Jesus commissions the apostles to heal and teach.)

Preparation

Decorate the church for Harvest but include cardboard clouds, a large golden sun and silver moon hung high up in the church where they can be easily seen if possible. Dress a boy in a habit to be St Francis. Have other youngsters ready to be the leper etc.

Presentation

Introduce 'St Francis' to the congregation before the Eucharist begins. Give a brief outline of his life and either recite or ask him to read part of the Canticle of the Sun. Lead straight into a version of this as the entrance hymn. 'All creatures of our God and King'.

Act out aspects of the life of Francis, using simple costumes if possible, before the readings. The creation reading can be linked with St Francis preaching to the birds or taming the wolf. The allusion to suffering in the Epistle can be linked with the episode of Francis receiving the marks of Christ's wounds (the stigmata) while at prayer. The Gospel can be prefaced by Francis praying in front of a crucifix and a gentle mention of his spiritual betrothal to 'Lady Poverty' and his life of consecration to God's service in celibacy.

Francis' care for the leper can be acted or mimed to introduce a brief homily on the 'lepers' of our own time, the handicapped, those without homes, those with AIDS, etc. The procession of Harvest gifts can then become an acted intercession – prayer leading to practical work for the kingdom.

St Francis' other well-known hymn, 'Make me a channel of your Peace' could be sung either during the sign of Peace or at Communion. Finally, the Blessing of St Francis can be given at the end of the liturgy.

This presentation does not attempt to portray the whole life of St Francis or even to follow the correct sequence. It picks up scenes from his life and relates them to the readings. With a little ingenuity this technique can be used with any story and readings.

12. Sending out the apostles

This is a mime to be acted during the reading of the Gospel about Jesus sending out 72 evangelists to proclaim the nearness of the Kingdom of God. The movements are simple and can be rehearsed in about 30 to 40 minutes. If the whole church area rather than just the chancel steps can be used, it adds to the effect of a journey being made.

Uses

• Any service about evangelization
• Feasts of Evangelists, especially St Luke
• ASB lectionary: Pentecost 5, Year 2
• Three-Year lectionary: 14th Sunday, Year C

Bible reading

Luke 10:1–12

Equipment

Each apostle needs to have a rucksack or similar bag, a purse – commonly known as a bum bag – and to be wearing flip-flop sandals. A basket with bread in it can be used by the people offering hospitality and a walking stick is a good symbol for the sick person.

Preparation

Five groups of people: apostles, waylayers, people in a welcoming village, sick people and unwelcoming people are needed. When rehearsing, give your actors clear directions about moving on a particular word or phrase in order to keep the action synchronized with the reading. If the reader cannot see the action clearly, have someone standing behind a pillar to direct any pauses or reminders of movement that are needed. This way, there is no need for lengthy rehearsal to ensure slick action.

Presentation

Place the apostles on the chancel steps with the other characters in pews, behind pillars, etc. Have the apostles dressed as suggested and standing in a row.

Movements during the narration:

v. 1   Move into pairs

v. 4   Take off and throw away bags. Kick off sandals. Walk forward. Waylayers move out to block the apostles with comments such as, 'Wait a minute!'
Apostles shake heads, point forward and keep walking.

v. 5   Stop at 'house', (i.e. a pew). Join in saying, 'Peace be with this house' and shake hands.

v. 7   Mime eating and drinking, passing round a bread basket, bottle etc.

v. 9   Sick people leap up and move off briskly.
Say together: 'The Kingdom of God has come near to you.'
With actions:
'The Kingdom of God' – put arms straight up and then out in a circle;
'has come' – put arms forward and beckon with hands.
'near to you' – fold hands on chest.

v.10   Unwelcoming people move into the apostles' way, making gestures of rejection, fold arms and turn their backs.

v.11   Apostles turn away, wiping feet on imaginary mat.
Return to chancel to be joined by other characters and all join in saying, 'The Kingdom of God has come near to you,' with actions as above.

13. Simultaneous Translation

This is a simple tableau to illustrate the reading from Acts 2 by relating it to modern technology. It is most effective if it is shown and described before the reading and then the characters stay 'frozen' during it.

Uses

- Pentecost Sunday
- Any liturgy about the power of the Holy Spirit

Bible reading

Acts 2

Equipment

- Several pairs of headphones from personal stereos.
- A few cards with names of countries on them – France, Brazil etc.

Preparation

Arrange some chairs and tables in a semicircle with a card in front of each place.

Presentation

Act out a 'United Nations' situation. Ask children to sit as 'delegates' at the table with another child wearing headphones standing behind each one to be a translator. Finally, put someone in front of the tables with a microphone to be the speaker.

Remind the children that they may have seen a situation like this on the news programmes. Explain how the speaker will speak in one language and the translators will simultaneously translate the speech into the delegates' own languages so that everyone hears and understands the speech at the same time. Point out that this is possible because we use skilled linguists and electronic equipment. We do not know *how* the people understood the Apostles' preaching on the first Pentecost Sunday but can imagine the effect to be similar to this.

14. The Way of the Cross with movement and actions

Uses

This could be used on Good Friday with the Stations of the Cross or as the Ministry of the Word at an all-age Eucharist in any setting, with or without Stations on the wall.

Bible readings

Any abbreviated version of the Passion story can be used or texts can be taken from one of the many books on the Stations of the Cross. If this is used as the whole Ministry of the Word, there will need to be readings as suggested below.

The traditional fourteen Stations of the Cross

1. Jesus is condemned to death	Matthew 27:20–26
2. Jesus takes up the cross	Matthew 27:27–31
3. Jesus falls the first time	Hebrews 2:17–18
4. Jesus meets his mother	Luke 1:30–33
5. Simon of Cyrene carries Jesus' cross	Matthew 27:32
6. Veronica wipes the face of Jesus	Matthew 25:35–40
7. Jesus falls the second time	Isaiah 53:5–6
8. The women weep for Jesus	Luke 23:33–34
9. Jesus falls the third time	1 Peter 2:22–24
10. Jesus is stripped of his garments	John 19:23–24
11. Jesus is nailed to the cross	Luke 23:33–34
12. Jesus dies on the cross	Luke 23:44–46
13. Jesus is taken down from the cross	John 19:38
14. Jesus is buried in the tomb	John 19:40–42

A further selection of Bible readings will be found in *Lent, Holy Week and Easter*.[6]

A shortened version can be enacted using Stations 1 and 2, then 11 to 14.

Preparation

It would be particularly effective to ask the children to make their own Stations from simple line drawings or collage work before the service. This could be part of the craft work in a Holy Week club or as the practical aspect of preparatory teaching on the Passion story. These could either be pinned up around the church or displayed at the front if it is not practical to move around during this presentation.

Presentation

Invite the children to become part of the story by performing an action at each Station. When Pilate washes his hands, they rub their palms together several times as a prayer is said. When Jesus receives his cross, they lay a hand on one of their own shoulders. When he falls, they kneel on one knee or two. When he is nailed to the cross, they stand with arms outstretched or make hammering gestures with clenched fists.

Music

Two popular modern hymns can be adapted with new words for singing between each Station:

Someone's judging, Lord,	Were you there when Pilate washed
kum ba yah (sung three times)	his hands? (twice)
Oh Lord, kum ba yah.	Oh, sometimes it causes me to
	tremble, tremble, tremble,
	Were you there when Pilate washed
	his hands?

Words that change at each verse:

1.	Judging	Pilate washed his hands?
2.	Wounded	He bore the wooden cross?
3.	Falling	He stumbled to the ground?
4.	Mourning	He met his mother's gaze?
5.	Helping	Simon shared his cross?
6.	Caring	She offered him her veil?
7.	Thirsty	He fell a second time?
8.	Crying	The women wept for him?
9.	Struggling	He struck the ground again?
10.	Lonely	The soldiers took his clothes?
11.	Suffering	He opened wide his arms?
12.	Dying	He bowed his head and died?
13.	Praying	They took him from the cross?
14.	Watching	They laid him in the tomb?

Sensitivity to the age and outlook of the children is required when deciding which actions to perform and which images to use. Selected Stations could be used as an extended Penitential rite during a Lenten all-age Eucharist. If care were taken to provide sufficient Scripture readings, with some Old Testament as well as Gospel passages, affirmation of faith and prayer for others, the Way of the Cross could form the whole Liturgy of the Word and then lead straight on to the Peace or Offertory.

15. What is coming? Who is coming?

These are two similar but separate activities which can used in the Advent Family Eucharist.

What is coming?

This audio presentation can illustrate a homily or introduce the theme of the Eucharist in the Advent season after the president has greeted the people.

Uses

- Any Sunday during the Advent season
- To set the scene on Advent Sunday, the Sunday when the Gospel presents John the Baptist or the Annunciation
- ASB Lectionary: Advent 3, Years 1 and 2; Advent 4, Year 1
- Three-Year Lectionary: Advent 3, Year A; Advent 2, 3 and 4, Year B; Advent 2 and 3, Year C

Bible readings

Any with the theme of the coming of the Messiah:
Mark 1:1–8; John 1:19–28 are especially appropriate.
Also Isaiah 7:10–14.

Equipment

- An audio cassette to be played through the church's sound system or on a portable cassette player.
- Record or tape of sound-effects, e.g. the BBC 'sound effects' series.

Preparation

Pre-record on the cassette a series of sounds which indicate that something is approaching, for example, an ambulance siren, a ship's foghorn, a racing car. End the recording with the sound of a crowd cheering.

Rehearse a group of children to say upon a cue, 'Jesus is coming, Jesus is coming ...', first quietly, then building up more loudly. Aim for a gradual increase of sound and excitement, not chanting.

Presentation

Play the tape, pausing to ask, 'What is coming?' after each sound. After the sound of cheering, ask, '*Who* is coming?' and let the children introduce the Advent message, 'Jesus is coming!' Though simple, this can be a strikingly effective way to set the Advent tone of expectancy.

Who is coming?

The second activity is a game to be played by young children to help them to get the idea of the excitement that the Jewish people felt when they were expecting the Messiah. It also illustrates the role of the prophets and John the Baptist in preparing the way of the Lord. It can be played as a game·during the children's own Ministry of the Word or acted out to illustrate teaching on the subject of preparation for Christ's coming.

Uses

- Any Sunday in Advent
- ASB Lectionary: Advent 2 and 3, Years 1 and 2
- Three-Year Lectionary: Advent 2 and 3, Years A and B, Advent 2, Year C

Bible readings

Isaiah 40:1–5
Matthew 3:1–12
Matthew 11:2–11 or 12–15
Mark 1:1–8
Luke 3:1–6
John 1:19–28

Equipment

- A cloak and crown for the king
- A length of red carpet – red crepe paper will do
- Anything to do with preparation for a Royal visit, flowers, flags to wave etc.
- A cheer-leader. This is best done by an adult or confident youngster with a louder voice than a child.

Preparation

Very little. If the children have played this game as part of their Advent activities, all they need to do is to act it again in church, maybe after a brief rehearsal to sort out the activities and props.

Presentation

Assemble the children at the side of the church near to the chancel, or, if the building is small, at the back of the church so that each child runs down the nave to the front.

A child runs forward calling out, 'The King is coming. I must dust the furniture' (or similar activity) and acts it out. Get each child to run forward in turn calling the same thing but with a different activity.

The last two children call out to the others, 'The King is coming, help us to lay out the red carpet.' They lay it along the nave and hand out a bunch of flags or streamers. Then either play a tape or ask the organist to play some grand music as the King comes forward from the back of the church to cheering, flag-waving, etc.

A brief talk or discussion afterwards should stress the kind of preparation that was needed to welcome the King, a clean, bright room and a clear way with a carpet, linking these with John the Baptist's message, 'Prepare the way of the Lord.'

References and suggested further reading

Chapter One: Principles

1   Children in the Way   National Society 1988

Chapter Two: Spirituality and worship

1   Stages of Faith, James W Fowler   Harper & Row 1981
    Becoming Adult, Becoming Christian,
    James W Fowler   Harper & Row 1984
2   How Faith Grows, Jeff Astley   National Society/CHP 1992
3   The Cognitive Development of Children,
    J Piaget   Routledge 1956
4   Religious Thinking from Childhood to
    Adolescence, R Goldman   Routledge 1964
5   The Spiritual Life of Children, Robert Coles   Harper Collins
                                                 1992

Chapter Three: Organization and planning

1   In Tune with Heaven   Hodder & Stoughton 1992
2   General Instruction on the Roman Missal
3   Directory of Children's Masses
4   The Alternative Service Book 1980   SPCK
5   Eucharistic Prayers for Masses with Children   Collins 1975
6   Lent, Holy Week and Easter   CHP 1989
7   The Promise of his Glory   CHP 1991

Chapter Four: Step by step through the Eucharist

1	The Sunday Missal – A New Edition	Collins 1982
2	The Promise of his Glory	CHP 1991
3	Hymns Old and New	Kevin Mayhew 1983
4	The Dramatised Bible	Harper Collins 1989
5	The Columba Lectionary for Masses with Children	Gracewing 1990
6	Song of Welcome for the Word, Christopher Walker; Music from the Mass, ed Bolton-Smith	Geoffrey Chapman 1985
7	The Sermon Slot vols 1&2, Sharon Swain	SPCK 1993
	Family Mass Themes, Sr Monica Mary	LSU Pastoral & Book Centre 1972
8	Mission Praise, Horrobin & Leavers	Marshall Pickering 1990

Chapter Five: Music

1	Music from Taizé vols 1&2, Jacques Berthier	Collins 1985
2	Wild Goose Songs, John L Bell and Graham Maule Heaven cannot wait etc	Wild Goose Publications 1987
3	Music from Lourdes, Paul Decha et al	Kevin Mayhew 1988
4	Come and Praise vols 1&2	BBC 1978
5	Someone's Singing, Lord Alleluia! Carol, Gaily Carol etc	A&C Black 1973, 1980, 1973
6	New People's Mass, Gregory Murray	Mayhew McCrimmon 1985
7	Music from the Mass vol 1, ed Geoffrey Boulton-Smith	Geoffrey Chapman 1985
8	Holy Trinity Service, Christopher Tambling Five more Parish Settings, Kevin Mayhew 1990	
9	Music for the Parish Communion, Martin How	RSCM 1984
10	Responsorial Psalter vols 1–3	McCrimmon 1988
11	Psalms for the Eucharist vols 1–3	Mayhew McCrimmon 1984

Chapter Six: Drama

1	Murder in the Cathedral, TS Eliot	Faber 1938
2	The little Flowers of St Francis, Blaiklock & Keys	Christian Classics, Hodder & Stoughton 1988

3   The Columba Lectionary for Masses with Children
                                    Gracewing 1990
4   The Dramatised Bible   Marshall Pickering 1989
5   Sketches from Scripture, Derek Haylock   CHP 1992
    Acts for Apostles   CHP 1987
6   Eh... Jesus ...Yes, Peter...? Seven dialogues,
    John L Bell and Graham Maule   Wild Goose Publications 1987
7   The Promise of his Glory   CHP 1991
8   Lent, Holy Week and Easter   CHP 1989
9   100+ Ideas for Drama; Another 100+ Ideas for Drama
    Anna Scher and Charles Verrall   Heinemann Educational 1989

Chapter Seven: Visual Aids

1   All God's Children?   National Society/CHP 1991
2   Saints, Signs and Symbols, W Ellwood Post   SPCK 1975
3   The Christmas Star, Malcolm Williamson   Joseph Weinberger
4   Short Cuts: Outline drawings of people and scenes from
    the Gospel stories   National Society/CHP 1989

Chapter Eight: Movement and Dance

1   Booklets of Folk Dances, English Folk Dance and Song Society,
            Cecil Sharpe House, 2 Regent Park Road, London, NW1
2   Steps of Faith; A practical introduction to Dance and Mime
                                    Kingsway 1984
3   Bright Ideas; Dance and Movement, Harrison, Layton and Morris
                                    Scholastic Publications 1989

Chapter Nine: Outreach

1   Meet Christ with Joy, Joan Brown   Kevin Mayhew 1991
2   Lifeline; a Confirmation course for young People,
            ed Pinchin & Wright, Church Literature Assn 1989
3   Calling You, Sharon J Swain   Mowbray 1992
4   Confirmation to follow, Stuart Thomas   Kevin Mayhew 1991
5   All Age Worship, Maggie Durran   Angel Press 1987
6   Keep it in the Family, Stuart Thomas   Kevin Mayhew 1993
7   Family Mass Themes, Sr Monica Mary
                        LSU Pastoral & Book Centre 1972

Chapter Ten: Ideas and illustrations

1 Saints, Signs and Symbols, W Ellwood Post   SPCK 1975
2 We always put a Candle in the Window, Marjorie Freeman
                                          National Society/CHP 1992
3 Frederick, Leo Leoni   Hodder and Stoughton 1971
4 The Complete Celebration Hymnal   McCrimmon 1991
5 Someone's Singing, Lord   A&C Black 1973
6 Lent, Holy Week and Easter   CHP 1989